PAUL MURPHY

1001 Dad Jokes: Making "Dad, Stop" the Official Family Motto

This book was professionally typeset on Reedsy.
Find out more at reedsy.com

Contents

Welcome to the 1001 Series!

You've just opened the first book in the **1001 Series**, packed with dad jokes, puns, and laughs. And the best part? There are plenty more books in the series, each one full of even more hilarious jokes, puns, and dad moments for you to enjoy.

There's also something for the whole family in the 1001 Series, so if you enjoy this book, check out the others for even more laughs, puns, and moments of pure comedy.

Find the rest of the **1001 Series** here:

- **Amazon UK**: amazon.co.uk/dp/B0DNR8WRM3
- **Amazon US**: amazon.com/dp/B0DNR8WRM3
- **Amazon Canada**: amazon.ca/dp/B0DNR8WRM3
- **Amazon Australia**: amazon.com.au/dp/B0DNR8WRM3

And yes, that's a zero after the B—it's not a typo, just Amazon's idea of a dad joke.

Now, let's get started—prepare for a journey of laughter, groaning, and undeniable dad joke brilliance.

You've Made It: The Dad Joke Hall of Fame

Congratulations! By picking up *1001 Dad Jokes*, you've taken the first step toward true greatness. If you're buying this book for yourself, welcome to the elite ranks of dad joke mastery—you're about to become unstoppable. But if you're buying this book for a dad, let us just say: **you're a true legend**. Seriously. You deserve a round of applause, a medal, and probably a statue in your honour. Your dad (or the dad you're gifting this to) will never forget this moment of pure brilliance. Trust us—they'll love it, even if everyone else groans.

Dad jokes are more than just bad puns. They're a sacred tradition, passed down from generation to generation like an embarrassing family heirloom. They're a way of life—a language spoken fluently by dads (and aspiring dads) everywhere, no matter their age, background, or level of dad-bod development. But most importantly, they're the quickest way to make someone smile—or roll their eyes so hard they see the back of their own skull.

Why write *1001 Dad Jokes*? Because the world needs it. We're here to arm you with the tools you need to brighten a dull moment, lighten a heavy mood, or successfully embarrass your kids in front of their friends. Whether you're a seasoned dad joke master or a rookie looking to up your pun game, this book is your ultimate resource.

What Can You Expect?

Jokes so funny, you'll be quietly shaking with laughter, hoping no one notices.

Puns so brilliant, everyone will secretly think you're a comedy genius.

Quips so quick, you'll be claiming whiplash.

Sarcasm so dry, it makes the Sahara look like a water park.

But here's the kicker: the 1001st joke in this book isn't just a joke—it's *the joke*. The crown jewel. The mic drop of dad humour. It's so good, we almost didn't include it. It's a belter. The kind of joke that makes you laugh, cry, and wonder why you didn't think of it first. Trust us—you're going to want to stick around for that one.

Your Mission, Should You Choose to Accept It

As you read, remember this: dad jokes are more than just words—they're moments. Moments of connection, laughter, and joy. They remind us that life doesn't have to be taken too seriously, and that sometimes the simplest jokes are the most meaningful.

So, grab a cup of coffee (or whatever fuels your humour), turn the page, and prepare to unleash 1001 jokes that will leave your audience groaning, laughing, or both. And remember: if they don't laugh the first time, just repeat the joke louder. That's the dad way.

The last page is calling you... but let's start with the first. Let's get pun-derway!

Parenting Perils

Parenting—where every day feels like you're competing on a reality show called *Survive the Chaos.* From negotiating bedtime treaties with toddlers to deciphering the ancient art of assembling a stroller, being a Dad is a full-contact sport.

This chapter dives into the unpredictable, hilarious, and sometimes sticky world of parenting. It's a tribute to all the Dads who've stepped on LEGO pieces, mastered the art of fake snoring during bedtime stories, and carried entire toy collections in their coat pockets. Parenting isn't always easy, but at least it's always entertaining. Let's laugh through the madness together!

1. How do I define bedtime?
It's the thing that starts 30 minutes before my kids 'finally' go to bed.

2. My kids asked why I never remember their friends' names.
I remember them perfectly—'Loud One', 'Hungry One' and '*That One*'.

3. Why do I still use the phrase "inside voices"?

Because it's my only hope for surviving kids' birthday parties.

4. Why do I never share my fries?
Because some things are sacred—even in parenting.

5. How do I survive bedtime stories?
By skipping pages like a ninja and praying they don't notice.

6. What's my secret weapon for surviving a day with kids?
Selective hearing—it's an essential dad skill.

7. My kids asked if they could have ice cream for breakfast.
I told them, "Sure, but only if you brush your teeth with sprinkles".

8. How do I know I'm a great dad?
Because no one else can pull off this level of organized chaos.

9. When the kids start a pillow fight, what's my next move?
Grab the biggest pillow and declare all out war.

10. My wife asked why I let the kids stay up late?
Because I'm preparing for a serious lie-in tomorrow.

11. What do I call it when I survive a tantrum in public?
A personal victory—and a reason to reward myself with a cold beer.

12. My kids told me I'm embarrassing.
I told them it's my job, and I'm due for a promotion.

13. How do I prepare for long car rides?

By mentally rehearsing how to answer "Are we there yet?" in at least five different ways.

14. My wife asked why I forget to pack the sunscreen.

Because we're only going to the park, not a desert safari!

15. My kids asked why I don't let them play with my tools.

Because I'm still recovering from the Great Glue Incident of 2020.

16. Why do I always agree to build pillow forts?

Because it's the closest I'll ever get to being an architect.

17. Why do I still check Halloween candy every year?

Because someone has to "test for poison"—especially the chocolate.

18. My wife asked why I never volunteer for school events.

Because I'd rather attend a lecture on the history of paperclips.

19. How do I know I'm raising smart kids?

They've already memorised the Wi-Fi password— I couldn't be prouder.

20. What's my least favourite part of parenting?

The bedtime negotiations—they're going to be lawyers.

21. My wife asked why I never put the bins out.

Because I'm convinced the bin day is just a conspiracy.

22. When my kids show me their art, what do I say?

"This belongs in a museum!"—one with a 'free entry, no judgement' policy.

23. How do I survive a kid's birthday party?

By hiding in the corner, pretending I'm just here for the cake.

24. What's the scariest sound in the house?

Silence—it usually means they're up to something terrifying.

25. How do I prepare for a kid's birthday party?

By carbo-loading like I'm running a marathon.

26. My wife asked why I always lose the grocery list.

It's the universe's way of making grocery shopping more exciting.

27. What's my go-to threat when the kids fight?

Turning off the Wi-Fi—instant peace treaty.

28. My kids asked why I always seem so calm.

Because I've mastered the art of pretending I'm not panicking inside.

29. When the kids perform at school, what do I do?

Cheer like it's the finals of a talent competition.

30. My wife asked why I let the kids watch TV during dinner.

Because it keeps them quiet long enough for me to eat.

31. Why do I still use baby talk with my kids?

Because it's the only voice they actually listen to.

32. How do I feel about playing video games with my kids?
Defeated—but at least they respect my effort.

33. My wife asked why I always wear the same jacket.
Because it's broken in, like my spirit.

34. When I lose a kid in the grocery store, what do I do?
Calmly call out, "Who wants ice cream?"—they appear instantly.

35. My wife asked why I let the kids eat on the couch.
Because crumbs are easier to clean than tantrums.

36. How do I survive school fundraisers?
By buying just enough to look supportive without going broke.

37. My kids asked why I always win at hide-and-seek.
Because I've turned hiding into a competitive sport and I'm in it to win it.

38. What's my strategy for family game night?
Trying to avoid the "I'm not playing with you anymore" meltdown.

39. My wife asked why I can't say "no" to puppy eyes.
Because they've mastered the Jedi mind trick.

40. Why do I always carry spare batteries?
Because I've got enough to deal with without adding a toy

battery crisis to my day.

41. My kids asked why I hate playgrounds.
Because climbing frames were not made for dads with bad knees.

42. How do I know I've become a real dad?
Because I groan every time I sit down—and it feels right.

43. My wife asked why I always buy the wrong size shoes.
Because kids' feet grow faster than my ability to shop.

44. Why do I pack extra socks wherever we go?
Because they vanish like magic tricks—and I'm not a magician.

45. When my kids asked why I can't keep up at the park, what did I say?
"Because my knees have an expiration date, and we're past it".

46. How do I handle a kid with a sugar rush?
By keeping a safe distance and wondering what I did to deserve this.

47. My wife asked why I let the kids pick dinner.
Because macaroni is less stressful than a mutiny.

48. Why do I always carry band-aids?
Because someone always needs one—even when they don't.

49. My kids asked why I still tell "dad jokes".
Because they're cheaper than therapy and twice as fun.

50. My wife asked why I let the kids eat dessert before dinner.
Because I'd rather deal with a sugar rush than a meltdown over broccoli.

As we cross the halfway mark in our parade of parenting pratfalls, let's take a moment to appreciate the quiet heroism of dadhood. This isn't just about mastering the art of stepping over toys without triggering a full-scale noise apocalypse; it's about celebrating those little victories, like finding a matching pair of socks on the first try or escaping a toddler's room without a creaky floorboard betrayal. So buckle up, grab your preferred snack (because, as we know, snacks are the secret weapon), and brace yourself for more side-splitting insights into the life of a dad. Because if parenting teaches us anything, it's that laughter is indeed the best way to navigate chaos.

51. Why do I always agree to play dress-up?
Because seeing myself as a fairy princess is the closest I'll ever get to royalty.

52. How do I make vegetable eating fun for my kids?
By calling broccoli "tiny trees" and telling them they're giants.

53. My wife asked why the kids' bath time is so chaotic.
Because they think they're training for the next Olympic

swimming team.

54. My kids asked why we can't have a pet dinosaur.
Because I'm not ready to deal with another creature that refuses to be potty trained.

55. Why do I look forward to school picture day?
Because it's the one day a year they don't look like they've been raised by wolves.

56. What's my technique for getting the kids to school on time?
Promising them a sneak peek at Christmas presents if we leave in the next five minutes.

57. How do I feel when I step on a LEGO?
Like I'm a wet bandit who didn't see the LEGO ambush coming.

58. My wife asked why I tell so many dad jokes.
Because I thrive on the sound of collective groaning.

59. When my kids ask why we have to recycle, what do I say?
Because we're saving the planet, one soda can and cardboard fort at a time.

60. Why am I considered the tickle monster?
Because no one escapes without a giggle.

61. My kids asked why they have a bedtime.
"Because my sanity is directly tied to your bedtime".

62. How do I get out of playing dolls again?
By pretending I'm a doll too and sitting quietly until they leave.

63. What's my strategy for peace during a sibling rivalry?
Declare myself the referee and then conveniently forget my whistle.

64. Why do I always lose at video games to my kids?
Because I was raised on joysticks, not thumbsticks.

65. My wife asked why the kids always come to me with maths homework.
Because I once solved a Sudoku and let it go to my head.

66. How do I get the kids to eat leftovers?
Tell them it's a new Pinterest recipe called "Deja Food".

67. What's my favourite part about playdates?
When they end and the house stops sounding like a zoo.

68. My kids asked why I never let them win races.
Because victory builds character—mine, not theirs.

69. Why do I pretend to love camping?
Because I get to say, "Back in my day, this was a luxury"—while secretly wishing for central heating.

70. What's my top parenting hack?
Telling the kids that the ice cream truck only plays music when it's out of ice cream.

71. How do I avoid sharing my dessert?

By pretending it fell on the floor—then eating it anyway.

72. My kids asked why we can't have a pool.

Because I'd have to sell the house to afford the water bill.

73. Why do I avoid school field trips?

Because I don't want to have to sneak off and hide in the toilet—crying my eyes out again.

74. My wife asked why I'm good at bedtime stories.

Because I can stretch a 30-minute story into a two-minute epic.

75. What's my trick to keep the kids quiet in the car?

Promising a 'mystery prize' at the next stop—if they stay quiet.

76. Why do I always walk into a room and forget why I'm there?

Because four hours of sleep turns me into a confused tourist in my own house.

77. My kids asked why I have gray hair.

told them each one represents a trip to the park with them, that ended in 'pure chaos'.

78. How do I keep my kids from getting bored at museums?

Make up wild stories about how I 'donated' half the artefacts.

79. Why do I cherish every moment with my children?

Because one day they'll stop arguing over who gets the last slice of pizza—and just take it without asking.

80. My wife asked why I'm always the one to fix toys.
Because every toy needs a hero, and I'm the only one that can save them.

81. What's my least favourite household chore?
Fishing crayons out of the washing machine.

82. Why do I encourage my kids to sing?
Because if they're singing, they're not asking questions.

83. My kids asked why I don't buy a faster car.
I'm saving my money for something even better—a one-way ticket to a tropical paradise with no bedtime sagas.

84. What's my parenting superpower?
Making up answers to impossible questions on the spot.

85. How do I deal with monsters under the bed?
Charge them rent—it's only fair.

86. My wife asked how I cope with the kids all day.
By imagining I'm surviving on a reality TV show called 'Dads vs. Kids', where the grand prize is a full night's uninterrupted sleep.

87. Why do I teach my kids to play chess?
Because it's quiet, strategic, and the pieces don't make a mess.

88. What's my secret to a calm house?

A good pair of noise-canceling headphones.

89. My kids asked why they can't watch more TV.

Because the TV needs to recover from all the rewinding, pausing, and fast-forwarding abuse.

90. Why do I encourage my kids to read comics?

Because I need someone else to understand my Batman references.

91. How do I convince my kids that chores are fun?

By telling them they're training for the World Championship of Domestic Disaster Relief—where the winner gets to call dibs on the TV remote, and the loser gets to finish their homework.

92. My wife asked why I always fall asleep during movies.

Because I'm just resting my eyes—during the entire film.

93. What's my favourite way to relax?

Pretend I'm looking for the kids while hiding in the shed.

94. Why do I love family game night?

It's the one time I'm allowed to be ruthlessly competitive.

95. How do I get the kids to do their homework?

Tell them it's a YouTube challenge.

96. My kids asked why I don't wear a cape.

Because superheroes need to blend in sometimes.

97. What's the best thing about being a parent?

Learning new ways to outsmart someone half your size.

98. Why do I always join in when they play on the trampoline?

Because I can't resist showing off my my gravity-defying moves.

99. My wife asked why I go all out for Halloween.

Because scaring the kids legally once a year is too good an opportunity to pass up.

100. What's the hardest part about parenting?

When they start asking real questions, and I don't have real answers.

Money Matters

Money—it's a Dad's favourite subject to pretend to understand. Whether it's debating the stock market (with zero stocks) or trying to explain interest rates to a kid who just spent their entire allowance on candy, we have a knack for turning finances into comedic gold.

This chapter is dedicated to all the Dads who've ever turned off lights in empty rooms while yelling, "I'm not made of money!" or convinced themselves that buying a new tool was 'an investment'. From budgeting blunders to accidental splurges, these jokes will prove that when it comes to finances, the real currency is laughter.

101. Why do I like doing the budget with my wife?

Because it's the one time we get to bond over our shared terror of credit card statements.

102. How do I explain taxes to the kids?

By eating 50% of their cookies and calling it "government sharing".

103. What's my wife's reaction when I try to fix the car myself to save money?

She secretly prepares herself to book a mechanic—knowing I'm about to create a whole new set of problems.

104. My mate asked why I invest in the stock market without understanding it.

I said, "It's adult gambling, but at least I get to blame the economy".

105. How do I teach my kids about money using board games?

By watching them turn Monopoly into a masterclass on how to bankrupt Dad.

106. What's my strategy when the boss talks about pay cuts?

Laugh and nervously say, "You almost had me there!"

107. How do I make budgeting fun for the kids?

By telling them the 'spending spy' is secretly watching them.

108. My boss asked why I drive a cheap car?

Expensive cars are for people who's 'performance-related bonus' is not a pat on the back.

109. What do I do when my kid asks for an allowance raise?

Give them a pat on the back.

110. What do I tell myself about saving for retirement?

I'm building a nest egg, but at this rate, the only surprise inside will be the faint echo of my financial dreams.

111. How do I justify a new power tool purchase to my wife?
"It's not spending, it's investing in home improvement!"

112. Why do I compare shopping for insurance to a marathon?
Both feel endless, and you need recovery time afterward.

113. What's the best financial advice I got from my boss?
"Diversify your portfolio"—but all I can afford to diversify is instant noodles.

114. What's my ultimate dad hack for saving money at the grocery store?
Pretending store-brand products taste better than name-brand.

115. My kids asked why I sigh when looking at bills.
I said it's grown-up yoga, helps me stay flexible about finances.

116. Why do I tell dad jokes about money at work?
Because a good pun is worth more than my retirement fund.

117. What's the game plan when I take my friends out for dinner?
Find the cheapest item on the menu and call it my favourite.

118. How do I explain our family budget to the kids?
It's like a video game where dad's wallet is the final boss.

119. Why do I take the boss's jokes about raises seriously?
Because pretending to believe it is part of the job description.

120. How do I convince my wife to save money?

I tell her all the shops are closed for a 'national budget awareness day'.

121. Why do my mates never ask me for financial advice?

Because they've seen me bargain with a vending machine.

122. What's my foolproof plan for financial stability?

Letting my loyalty card points accumulate until I can afford a free coffee.

123. How do I deal with expensive hobbies according to my wife?

By calling them 'investments' and hiding the receipts.

124. Why do I involve the kids in home economics?

Because they need to learn why dad's always turning off lights.

125. What's my response when my friend brags about his stocks?

Just wait till my kid's lemonade stand goes public!

126. Why do I love payday?

Because I get to pretend I'm rich for two glorious hours

127. How do I turn a work bonus into a teachable moment at home?

Explain that sometimes, the treasure chest is just enough to cover the leaky roof.

128. What did my boss say when I asked for a raise?
"How about a high five instead?"

129. How do I encourage my kids to save money?
By explaining that saving is like eating your vegetables—good for you, but you won't see the benefits immediately.

130. Why do I get nostalgic about old credit card bills?
Because they take me back to a time when they were a backup, not a lifeline.

131. What's my best trick for dealing with a tight month?
Invite myself to dinner at a friend's house—weekly.

132. Why do I consider lottery tickets a solid investment?
Because I'm diversifying my portfolio, one scratch-off at a time

133. How does my wife react when I splurge on tech?
She finds a way to deduct it from my future allowance.

134. What's my go-to strategy for saving on kids' toys?
Wait until they forget about them, then re-gift at Christmas.

135. Why do I love listening to financial podcasts?
Because misery loves company, especially in traffic.

136. How do I explain mortgage interest to my kids?
"It's like buying a pizza but paying for each slice every month for 30 years".

137. Why am I the designated bill payer in the house?

Because I've got the best poker face when it comes to seeing how much is due.

138. What's my take on investing in gold?

My budget's stuck on silver.

139. How do I motivate myself to review the finances?

By treating it like a mystery novel—where I need to find out where all the money went.

140. How does my Wife react to my 'new business idea'?

Nods enthusiastically, but she's already mentally preparing herself for the next 'big idea'.

141. Why did I call an 'emergency' family budgeting meeting?

Because the credit card bill looked more like a novel than a statement.

142. How do I deal with high energy bills?

Tell ghost stories about the electric meter—to scare the kids into turning off lights.

143. What's my kids' idea of financial planning?

Making a list of toys they want and calling it a 'vision board'.

144. How does my boss contribute to my financial planning?

By inspiring me to look up side hustles while pretending to care about quarterly projections.

145. What do I consider a financial win?

When I resist the urge to buy snacks at the petrol station.

146. Why do I teach my kids poker?

To prepare them for the high-stakes game of deciding who gets the last slice of pizza.

147. What's my favourite financial philosophy?

Life's short—buy it now and figure out how to pay for it later.

148. Why do I bring my kids shopping?

I like to think of kids' parking as one of my personal 'dad perks'.

149. What's my secret to saving for vacation?

Cook tropical meals at home and call it an all-inclusive staycation.

150. How does my wife make budget cuts fun?

She gamifies it by giving bonus points for reusing gift bags.

You've made it halfway—think of it as surviving a budget meeting with toddlers: exhausting, surprising, and somehow still fun. The first 50 jokes were like the free samples; now we're hitting the premium content—no coupons required. Dads have a knack for turning financial chaos into comedy gold, whether it's claiming the broken dishwasher was 'an investment in family bonding time' or convincing the kids that eating leftovers is a 'money-saving adventure'. From impulse buys to unexpected expenses (usually caused by said impulse buys), this is where dad-finance logic truly shines. So, tighten your imaginary wallet, adjust your humour budget, and let's dive back in. Just remember, everything is negotiable... except snack money.

151. My kids asked why we can't just print more money.
I said, "Because the government won't let me borrow their printer".

152. Why does my wife handle the online shopping?
Because I once bought a bread maker while shopping for a toaster.

153. What's my boss's favourite budgeting advice?
"Do more with less". I told him I've already mastered that with my salary.

154. How do I teach my kids about loans?
By giving them a 'payment holiday' when they're extra well-behaved.

155. My mate asked why I always buy generic brands.
Because I don't need sparkling water endorsed by a Kardashian.

156. Why do I get nervous around cash machines?
Because they make my bank balance feel like a public humiliation.

157. How do I justify buying coffee at work every day?
By calling it my "productivity fuel investment".

158. My wife asked why I keep old receipts.
Because they're like diary entries for all my financial regrets.

159. Why do I never buy the extended warranty?
Because warranties are like mates who vanish the second you need help.

160. How do I decide what to splurge on?
If it's shiny or has an app, I'll find a reason.

161. My kids asked why we don't go on holiday more often.
I told them we do—why fly to Spain when we've got a picnic bench in the garden?

162. Why does my boss call me "thrifty"?
Because I charge my phone at work to save on electricity.

163. My wife asked how I plan to save more money.
By only buying things with yellow discount stickers on them.

164. Why do my mates laugh when I offer financial advice?
Because they know I've got a PhD in creative spending.

165. What's my foolproof method for saving money?
Avoiding eye contact with my kids in the toy aisle.

166. How do I explain stocks to my wife?
It's like lending a mate money and hoping he doesn't blow it all on snacks.

167. Why do I always bring a shopping list?

Because otherwise, I'd end up with three kinds of cheese and no bread.

168. What's my financial motto?

If it's free, it's for me.

169. My mate asked how I plan to retire.

I told him my strategy is simple: win the lottery.

170. Why does my wallet look like it's bursting?

Because I never throw away a voucher, even if it's expired.

171. My wife asked why I bought another gadget.

Because it was 20% off, which technically means I saved money.

172. How do I prepare for Christmas?

By subtly suggesting socks as the ultimate gift idea.

173. My kids asked why they can't have a credit card.

Because they'd probably max it out on pizza and Pokémon cards.

174. What's my biggest financial achievement?

Convincing the dog to stop chewing the furniture—it saved us a fortune.

175. Why does my boss think I'm 'resourceful'?

Because I used a rubber band to keep the office door open during a heatwave.

176. My mate asked how I stay so optimistic about money.
Because I've mastered the art of ignoring my bank balance.

177. How do I convince my kids to save their pocket money?
By declaring myself their "money mentor" and charging a consultation fee.

178. Why do I never win at poker night?
Because I celebrate too early when I get a pair of twos.

179. My wife asked why I keep promising to fix things.
Because it buys me time to Google how to actually do it.

180. How do I know my kids are growing up?
They've started asking about investing—mainly in sweets.

181. My boss asked what motivates me to work harder.
I've got a lot of streaming subscriptions to pay for.

182. Why do I use cash instead of cards?
Because nothing feels more real than physically handing over regret.

183. My mate asked why I never buy new cars.
I told him, "Because depreciation happens faster than my decision-making".

184. What's my strategy for holiday souvenirs?
Take photos—it's free and doesn't require extra luggage.

185. How do I explain credit to my kids?

It's like borrowing a toy, but if you break it, the penalty is five times its value.

186. My wife asked why I compare deals obsessively.

Because finding the cheapest price is my version of a sport.

187. What's my biggest financial weakness?

Walking past a DIY store without buying something 'essential'.

188. Why do I keep my old wallet?

Because a new wallet feels unnecessary when there's nothing to put in it.

189. My kids asked why I groan at utility bills.

Because I'm pretty sure the heating's running a secret side hustle.

190. What's my dream financial scenario?

A month where my income lasts longer than my expenses.

191. My boss asked why I never turn off lights before leaving work.

Because I'm secretly trying to get us into the Guinness World Records for electricity usage.

192. How did I resist buying snacks at the petrol station?

I looked at the price and thought, 'Is this a snack or a down payment on a car?'

193. Why do I hate online shopping with my wife?

Because every time we find a bargain, it turns into an emergency purchase.

194. What's my ultimate budgeting hack?
Convincing everyone it's fun to stay home.

195. My kids asked why they have to earn their pocket money.
Because the only thing I hand out for free is bad advice.

196. Why do I love cashback schemes?
It's my favourite form of getting a little something back from the chaos of shopping.

197. My wife asked why I want to invest in a shed.
It's my retreat—where I can escape the responsibility of being an adult.

198. What's my excuse when I overspend?
I'm just providing a case study in the perils of online shopping.

199. Why do I avoid talking finances with friends?
Because I'm still pretending I understand what an ISA is, and I don't need anyone calling me out.

200. How do I make my kids respect money?
Give them a coin and say, "This is your inheritance, spend it wisely".

Tech Troubles

Ah, technology—the one thing in life designed to keep Dads humble. Whether it's accidentally turning on the flashlight instead of answering a call or loudly demanding, "What's the Wi-Fi password?" while it's written on the router, we've all been there.

This chapter dives into the hilarity of Dads vs. tech, a battle where the machines often win but we never stop trying. From fighting the printer to staring suspiciously at the cloud (both the weather kind and the storage kind), these jokes will remind you that tech support isn't just a job—it's a Dad's lifelong destiny. So grab your smartphone (if you can figure out how it works) and let's scroll through some laughs.

201. What's my biggest win with technology?
   Getting the voice assistant to understand me.

202. My kids caught me staring at the Wi-Fi router.
   I told them I was 'mentally resetting it'.

203. How do I explain the cloud to my wife?

It's like a virtual attic—just without the creepy boxes and spiders.

204. My boss asked why I missed the Zoom call?

"I got lost in the virtual waiting room".—But really, I didn't want to be seen in my underpants.

205. My mate asked how I fixed the printer jam.

I said, "With patience, determination, and a little bit of yelling".

206. Why do I keep closing tabs on the browser?

Because I'm trying to conserve digital space—for no logical reason.

207. How do I manage to lock myself out of my own laptop?

It's simple: I forget the password and refuse to admit it.

208. What's my approach to fixing a smart thermostat?

Act confused, press random buttons, and call it a day.

209. My wife asked why I always forget the Wi-Fi password.

I believe in living in the moment, not being tied down by things like passwords.

210. When the TV freezes, what do I do?

I give it a motivational speech: 'Come on, you've got this. Just one more episode!

211. How do I handle pop-up ads?

By frantically clicking 'X' and accidentally opening three

more windows.

212. My mate asked why I don't trust smart speakers.
Because they know more about my life than I do.

213. What's my trick for video calls?
Just freeze mid-sentence... and see how long it takes before someone says, "Are you okay?"

214. When my kids asked why I say "www" before websites, what did I tell them?
I say it to let the computer know I'm coming in hot!

215. My work colleague asked how I always manage to mute myself during meetings.
It's a survival skill—which I've perfected over several years of marriage.

216. What's the scariest tech phrase I've ever heard?
"Firmware update".

217. My boss asked why I use two monitors?
One's for work, and one's for googling how to do the work.

218. My mate laughed when I said I still keep old cables.
But who'll be have the last laugh when he needs a charger for his Nokia 3210?

219. How do I explain autocorrect to my kids?
It's a tool that makes your mistakes even funnier.

220. When the printer stopped working, what did I do?

Paced the room dramatically until it printed out of fear.

221. Why do I always click "later" on software updates?

I'm busy with more important things... like scrolling through cat videos.

222. What's my secret weapon for fixing tech issues?

Turning it off, waiting 10 seconds, and pretending I'm a genius when it works.

223. My mate asked why I still carry wired headphones.

Because Bluetooth is for people who don't appreciate a good challenge.

224. How do I prepare for updates?

By mentally saying goodbye to whatever worked before.

225. When my kids asked why I call apps 'programs', what did I say?

Because that's what the cool dads called them in the 90s.

226. My boss asked why I avoid digital signatures.

Because signing with a mouse feels like trying to draw with a sausage.

227. When the TV remote disappeared, what did I do?

Blamed the dog—it's the only logical explanation.

228. How do I survive a day with no internet?

By telling myself it's 'retro day' and reading the back of cereal boxes.

229. My wife asked why I still buy DVDs.
Because streaming buffers, but DVDs never let me down.

230. What's my favourite part about autocorrect?
It's like having a mischievous gremlin edit my texts.

231. My kids asked how I deal with tech support.
By describing the problem dramatically and hoping they feel sorry for me.

232. When my boss asked why my emails are late, what did I say?
"I needed to make sure they were perfect... eventually".

233. My mate asked why I won't try smart watches.
Because I don't need another gadget judging my every move.

234. What's my approach to remembering passwords?
Guess until I accidentally get it right.

235. My wife asked how I keep breaking the smart TV.
Because I'm 'testing its limits'.

236. How do I explain 4K resolution to my kids?
It's like regular TV, but now you can count everyone's wrinkles.

237. When the Wi-Fi stopped working, what did I do?
Blamed the weather, the kids and dog. Never the router itself.

238. My mate asked why I still keep a landline.

Because it never runs out of battery.

239. What's the hardest part about updates?

Accepting that things might work differently... or not at all.

240. How do I troubleshoot a frozen tablet?

By mimicking its behaviour and refusing to respond.

241. My boss asked why I don't use the company's apps.

Because they're as user-friendly as a brick wall.

242. My kids asked why I yell at loading screens?

Basic Dad Logic—yelling speeds things up.

243. My wife asked why I always restart the router.

Because turning it off and on again is the closest thing to magic I know.

244. What's my favourite tech phrase?

"Your device needs an update"—said no one ever.

245. How do I explain QR codes to my parents?

It's like a barcode, but this one actually does something interesting.

246. My mate asked why I don't use emojis.

Because words worked fine for Shakespeare, so they're good enough for me.

247. My wife asked why I carry three chargers?

I'm preparing for the apocalypse—or a family trip.

248. What's my reaction to a frozen phone?
Shake it gently and hope it thaws.

249. My kids asked why I don't trust Bluetooth.
Because it never connects unless I don't need it to.

250. My mate asked why I use two-factor authentication?
Because three-factor sounds exhausting.

Well done, you've made it halfway through the minefield of Dad vs. Technology! That's no small feat—kind of like successfully printing double-sided without a meltdown. The first 50 jokes were just the loading screen; now we're diving deeper into the hilarious chaos of apps that crash, Wi-Fi that disappears at the worst possible moment, and the eternal mystery of why the TV remote is always in the fridge. Dads may never truly conquer tech, but that won't stop us from trying... and loudly blaming the router along the way. So, power up for round two—just make sure the kids don't take over your 'tech support' title before we're done.

251. My kids caught me yelling at the TV remote again.
It's the only thing in the house that doesn't talk back.

252. How do I handle slow internet?
By pacing the room like a tech support operator waiting for a miracle.

253. My wife asked how I keep losing the Wi-Fi password.

I told her it's part of my exercise routine—running back to the router.

254. What's my strategy for fixing the printer?

Unplug, replug, and pray to the tech gods.

255. My mate said I need to let go of my fax machine.

I told him, "Some traditions are worth keeping, even if no one else agrees".

256. Why do I always mess up text messages?

Because my thumbs are about as graceful as a toddler on roller skates.

257. My kids asked if I even know how to use their tablet.

Of course I do—it's the thing I accidentally lock every time I touch it.

258. When the TV freezes, what do I do?

Stare at it harder, hoping my disappointment will reboot it.

259. My boss asked why my emails are always late.

Because spellcheck takes its sweet time roasting me first.

260. How do I explain QR codes to my kids?

It's like a barcode but with more attitude.

261. My wife caught me trying to fix the router again.

She doesn't understand—it's a battle of wills, and I refuse to lose.

262. What's the most terrifying thing about autocorrect?

It knows my weaknesses and uses them against me.

263. My mate asked how I still manage to lock myself out of my phone.

It's a skill I've honed through years of forgetting my own patterns.

264. Why do I always squint at my laptop screen?

Because I'm trying to see the pixels conspiring against me.

265. My kids asked why I keep closing apps.

Because it's the closest I'll ever get to tidying up a mess.

266. What's my biggest tech fear?

Getting stuck in an endless loop of 'Forgot Password?'.

267. My wife asked why I carry three chargers everywhere.

Because tech failures love to strike when you're unprepared.

268. How do I handle a frozen tablet?

By freezing myself until one of us gives in.

269. My boss asked why I never use the company's online tools.

Because they require a PhD in frustration.

270. My mate asked what I think about voice assistants.

I think they're secretly judging me for not knowing what I'm doing.

271. Why do I keep my old flip phone?
Because it's indestructible, unlike my patience with smartphones.

272. My kids asked why I call their video games 'distractions'.
Because I can't seem to win at them, and I hate losing.

273. How do I handle an accidental screen rotation?
By tilting my head and pretending it's not happening.

274. My wife asked how I manage to butt-dial so often.
Because my pockets are smarter than my brain.

275. What's my solution when an app won't work?
Delete it and claim victory—then reinstall it five minutes later.

276. My boss asked why my screen is so cluttered.
I told him, "It's organised chaos. Mostly chaos".

277. My mate laughed at my 'low-tech' solutions.
But duct tape and determination always win in the end.

278. Why do I still write down my passwords?
Because my memory is a sieve, and the cloud doesn't do sticky notes.

279. My kids asked how I take so many blurry photos.
Because I'm an artist, not a tripod.

280. What's the hardest part about using new tech?

Admitting that the kids were right all along.

281. My wife asked why I keep deleting her apps.
I told her it's not sabotage—it's spring cleaning.

282. How do I explain 4K TVs to my parents?
"It's like regular TV, but now you can see all the pores".

283. My mate asked why I still buy gadgets.
Because hope is a powerful motivator, even for bad purchases.

284. My boss asked how I still use WordArt.
I told him it's called "retro charm".

285. What's my trick for staying calm during updates?
Staring at the progress bar like it's my nemesis.

286. My kids asked why I use dark mode on everything.
Because it matches my soul after trying to set up the Wi-Fi.

287. My wife caught me yelling at the microwave clock again.
To be fair, it started it.

288. Why do I avoid apps that track my steps?
Because the last thing I need is another source of judgement.

289. My boss asked why I still don't digital signatures.
Because signing with a mouse feels like finger painting with boxing gloves.

290. My mate asked how I still get lost with GPS.

I told him it's not me—it's the satellites playing tricks.

291. My kids asked why I always use the wrong emoji.
Because every button looks like a mystery waiting to be solved.

292. My wife asked how I still confuse the USB cables.
I told her they're like identical twins who hate me equally.

293. What's my number one rule for fixing tech?
If it's not working, slap it gently and hope for the best.

294. My mate asked why I don't trust Bluetooth.
Because it never connects when you need it most.

295. My boss asked why I avoid tech training sessions.
Learning is hard, pretending I already know is easy.

296. How do I handle a dead phone battery?
By dramatically announcing that "I'm off the grid".

297. My kids asked why I'm so bad at video games.
Because I grew up playing Pong.

298. My wife asked why I buy gadgets I never use.
Because they look good collecting dust.

299. How do I survive bad Wi-Fi?
By blaming everything on the weather.

300. My work colleague asked why I still use a wired mouse.
Because I'm secretly a time traveller from the pre-Bluetooth

era.

DIY Disasters

Welcome to the world of DIY—where Dads transform simple home projects into epic sagas of trial and error. Armed with nothing but overconfidence and a set of Allen wrenches, we dive head first into assembling furniture, fixing leaks, and creating masterpieces that inevitably require professional help to undo.

This chapter celebrates those glorious moments when 'measure twice, cut once' turns into "whoops, better buy more wood." Whether it's shelves that lean like the Tower of Pisa or light fixtures that only work on leap years, these jokes are a tribute to every Dad who's ever proudly declared, "I got this", just before realizing he absolutely does not.

301. My wife asked why I keep buying power tools.
They're trophies for projects I haven't started yet.

302. How do I know my DIY project is not going well?
When the dog leaves the room in fear.

303. My wife asked why haven't fixed the leaky tap.
Because I'm pretty sure the tap's just going through a phase.

304. What's my motto when assembling flat-pack furniture?
Measure once, panic twice.

305. My kids asked why I have so much duct tape.
Because it's cheaper than therapy and fixes nearly as much.

306. How do I handle instructions in DIY kits?
By ignoring them entirely and relying on my Dad instincts.

307. My wife asked why I refuse to call a plumber.
Because admitting defeat is not part of my skill set.

308. What's my strategy for hanging pictures straight?
Eyeballing it, followed by denial.

309. My mate asked why my toolbox weighs so much.
Because it's filled with dreams, regrets, and a lot of spare screws.

310. Why do I always have leftover parts after a project?
Because those are 'bonus pieces' for next time.

311. My wife asked why the garden shed has two doors.
One for getting in, and one for dramatically storming out when I can't find the tools.

312. How do I know I've overcomplicated a project?
When the kids look at me like I've lost my mind.

313. My kids asked why the swing set wobbles.
Because I wanted to give them an extra thrill.

314. My mate asked why I don't use a level.
Because leaning shelves have character.

315. What's my secret to fixing leaks?
Strategic buckets and a lot of crossed fingers.

316. My wife asked why the paint job looks streaky.
Because I was aiming for a 'rustic charm' vibe.

317. How do I explain the hole in the wall?
"It's ventilation. Very modern".

318. My mate asked why I keep every nail and screw.
They're for my future DIY empire!

319. What's my go-to DIY advice?
Start big and figure out the details later.

320. My wife asked why I installed the curtain rod upside down.
Because 'creative choices' are a key part of my brand.

321. How do I handle assembling furniture with missing pieces?
By improvising and pretending it was part of the plan.

322. My kids asked why their bunk bed creaks so much.
It's auditioning for a role in a horror movie— "The Haunted Bunk Bed".

323. My mate asked why I keep painting over mistakes.

I prefer to think of it as 'abstract art'.

324. What's my plan for fixing a squeaky door?

Ignore it until it fixes itself.

325. My wife asked why the new shelf is tilted.

It's leaning into the future—just ahead of its time.

326. How do I feel about following safety instructions?

Like they're optional challenges for the overconfident.

327. My mate asked why I always have an emergency plank of wood.

You never know when you might need to build a raft.

328. My kids asked why their tree house doesn't have a roof.

Because 'natural airflow' builds character.

329. What's my approach to rewiring a light fixture?

Step 1: Turn off the power. Step 2: Panic. Step 3: Hope for the best.

330. My wife asked why the new table wobbles.

Because 'adjustable stability' is trendy.

331. How do I measure things accurately?

By guessing and hoping for the best.

332. My mate asked why my fence has a gap.

I like to think of it as a 'peekaboo' feature for the neighbours.

333. My kids asked why the trampoline is lopsided.
It's just practising its 'leaning tower of trampoline' look.

334. My wife asked why I insist on fixing everything myself.
Because Dad pride outweighs practicality.

335. How do I know a project is getting out of hand?
When I'm on my fifth trip to the hardware store.

336. My mate asked why I installed the door backwards.
Because it's accessible design for vampires.

337. My wife asked why the new cabinet doesn't open properly.
It's just shy—it'll open up once it gets to know us better.

338. How do I feel about power saws?
Like they're both my best friend and my mortal enemy.

339. My kids asked why the doghouse leaks.
It's a fixer-upper, just like the rest of my DIY projects.

340. My wife asked why the bathroom tiles are crooked.
It's called 'modern asymmetry'—very trendy these days.

341. What's my ultimate DIY philosophy?
If it looks fine from a distance, it's perfect.

342. My mate asked why I built a birdhouse without a roof.
It's a starter home—great for birds on a budget.

343. How do I handle broken furniture?

With duct tape, super glue, and blind optimism.

344. My wife asked why the picture frame keeps falling.
Because I'm testing gravity in real time.

345. My kids asked why the tree house stairs are so steep.
It's a fitness feature—you'll thank me later!

346. My mate asked why my workbench is always messy.
Because chaos inspires creativity.

347. My wife asked why the ceiling fan is wobbling.
It's showing off its 'freestyle spin' mode.

348. How do I know I've finished a project?
When I've run out of excuses.

349. My kids asked why the sandbox is full of water.
It's an impromptu beach experience.

350. My mate asked why I keep starting new projects.
It's my way of showing I'm a visionary, not a completer.

Congratulations, you've hammered, drilled, and duct-taped your way to the halfway mark! Like any great Dad project, it hasn't been smooth—there have been plenty of uneven shelves, questionable measurements, and 'temporary fixes' along the way. But isn't that the charm of DIY? This is the point where the real fun begins, where overconfidence meets reality, and every project feels one trip to the hardware store away from greatness. So grab your Allen wrench, take a deep breath, and let's see what other disasters we can turn into 'character-building experiences' in the second half!

351. My wife asked why I needed a laser level.
Because it sounds cool, and now I feel like a secret agent.

352. How do I know my DIY skills are improving?
Fewer things fall over when I leave the room.

353. My mate asked why I used so much wood glue.
Because when in doubt, glue it out!

354. My kids asked why the birdhouse is on the ground.
Because the birds requested a bungalow.

355. What's my go-to fix for a stuck drawer?
Brute force followed by blaming the manufacturer.

356. My wife asked why I installed the shower head so high.
I wanted to make sure even NBA players feel welcome here.

357. How do I prepare for painting a wall?
I stare at it for an hour and then decide it's a job for tomorrow.

358. My mate asked why I built a bench that creaks.
It's not a creak; it's an audible feature for added character.

359. My kids asked why the dog's new ramp is so steep.
I thought it'd make fetch a bit more exciting.

360. What's my secret to assembling flat-pack furniture?
Pure stubbornness and the occasional swear word.

361. My wife asked why I replaced the garden hose.
It's not a replacement—it's an upgrade to my watering game.

362. My mate asked how I made a table that wobbles on carpet.
That, my friend, is a skill.

363. How do I explain the missing fence post?
It's on holiday.

364. My kids asked why the new slide has a sharp turn.
It's a built-in test of bravery—only the bold make it to the bottom.

365. My wife asked why I buy extra screws for every project.
Because I lose 50% of them before finishing.

366. What's my excuse when the light fixture falls?
Now it's easier to reach!

367. My mate asked why I always overbuy wood.
Because running out mid-project is the ultimate Dad failure.

368. My wife asked why the curtain rod keeps falling.
Because the wall doesn't respect my authority.

369. How do I know when a DIY project is a disaster?
When the kids start taking bets.

370. My kids asked why their bunk bed squeaks.

It's not squeaking—it's singing a bedtime lullaby!

371. My wife asked how I managed to paint the ceiling by accident.

The roller had dreams of going higher, and I didn't stop it

372. What's my approach to fixing a leaky pipe?

Call it 'controlled water flow' and hope for the best.

373. My mate asked why I can't just hire a professional.

Because where's the fun in watching someone else struggle?

374. My kids asked why the playhouse has no windows.

I'm saving the windows for the sequel—Playhouse 2.0

375. My wife asked why I keep breaking drill bits.

Because I'm testing their durability—for science.

376. How do I survive trips to the hardware store?

I mentally prepare for the debate between 'which screw is better'.

377. My mate asked why my shelves are so shallow.

They're designed for displaying my achievements.

378. My kids asked why their tree house door doesn't close.

It's not a door; it's a very fancy air vent.

379. My wife asked why the new bench is lopsided.

Because it's a conversation piece.

380. How do I deal with a missing hammer?

Borrow someone else's and pretend it was mine all along.

381. My mate asked why my DIY workbench is wobbly.

It's just practising its earthquake preparedness.

382. My wife asked why I keep buying extra nails.

I'm starting a nail collection. Very exclusive.

383. My kids asked why the sandbox is tilted.

It's not tilted—it's a natural sand dune experience!

384. My mate asked why I don't measure properly.

Because measuring feels like cheating.

385. How do I handle a crooked shelf?

Convince everyone it's abstract.

386. My wife asked why the new dining table won't fit in the kitchen.

I thought we could eat half the meal in the kitchen and half in the hallway.

387. My kids asked why the swing set leans.

Because a bit of danger keeps things exciting.

388. My mate asked why I have three toolboxes.

One's for tools, one's for 'missing' tools, and one's for tools I'll never use.

389. How do I explain the extra holes in the wall?

They're ventilation points... very trendy these days.

390. My wife asked why the deck looks unfinished.
I ran out of wood and enthusiasm at the same time.

391. My mate asked how I managed to glue my hand to a project.
I get too attached to my work—occupational hazard.

392. My kids asked why their new desk wobbles.
I wanted to make sure you stay awake while doing homework.

393. My wife asked why the garden gate swings the wrong way.
The gate and I had a difference of opinion, and it won.

394. What's my plan for fixing squeaky stairs?
Convince everyone that squeaks are part of the house's charm.

395. My mate asked why I keep buying paint rollers.
Because the old ones are still in 'paint rehab' after my last project.

396. My wife asked why the bathroom tiles don't match.
The tiles wanted to express themselves, and I respected that.

397. My kids asked why the tree house ladder is so short.
It's a tree house, not a penthouse—short ladders are part of the charm!

398. My mate asked why I keep starting new projects.

Because finishing them would ruin my brand.

399. My wife asked why the gutter is crooked.

It's a feature—now we have a built-in water slide for rain!

400. How do I explain the half-painted wall?

I'm letting the other half of the wall appreciate what's coming.

School Days

Ah, school days—a time of learning, laughter, and finding out just how much glitter a single art project can generate. As Dads, we're the unsung heroes of homework help, carpool chaos, and navigating the mysteries of modern education (seriously, when did maths start needing the alphabet?).

This chapter is a nostalgic nod to the glory days of recess, packed lunches, and trying to convince your teacher that the dog really did eat your homework. From class field trips to parent-teacher conferences, these jokes prove that school isn't just for kids—it's also a goldmine of hilarity for parents.

401. My kids asked why I always pack too many snacks for school trips.
Because hungry kids are scarier than the trip itself.

402. How do I handle maths homework?
I start by Googling the answers and pretending I knew all along.

403. My wife asked why I signed up for the bake sale.

Because I thought 'bake sale' was code for buying cupcakes.

404. What's my favourite part of the school run?

When it's over.

405. My kids asked why I always make them wear jumpers to School.

It's like a protective layer for all the stains you're about to collect.

406. My wife asked why I get nervous at parent-teacher conferences.

It's not easy being told your kid is just as 'spirited' as you were.

407. How do I handle permission slips?

I sign them so fast, I don't even read what I'm agreeing to.

408. My wife asked how the field trip went?

It was great! I only lost three kids... just kidding, they found me.

409. What's my reaction to glitter-covered art projects?

Beautiful! Now where's the vacuum?

410. My kids asked why I can't help with science homework.

Because I'm still recovering from when Pluto stopped being a planet.

411. My mate asked why I dread school fundraisers.

Because 'fun' in fundraiser is a lie!

412. How do I explain algebra to my kids?

It's like solving a mystery where the villain is the letter X.

413. My wife asked why I always forget the PE kit.

Because it's tradition at this point—why break the streak?

414. What's my survival tactic for class assemblies?

Clap enthusiastically and hope it ends quickly.

415. My kids asked why I pack boring sandwiches.

Because sandwiches shaped like dinosaurs are a weekend luxury.

416. My mate asked why I never compete in school sports day.

I'd hate to overshadow the kids with my world-class egg-and-spoon technique.

417. How do I feel about helping with school projects?

Like I should get an honorary degree for my glue gun skills.

418. My wife asked why I don't help with the kids' homework more often.

I don't want to risk proving I'm worse at maths than a 10-year-old.

419. What's my trick for helping the kids find lost school books?

I dramatically check the fridge.

420. My kids asked why I cheer so loudly at sports day.

Loud cheers scare off the competition—it's all part of the

strategy.

421. My mate asked how I survive school discos.
I hang out by the snack bar.

422. What's my approach to art homework?
I provide moral support... from a safe distance.

423. My wife asked why I forget picture day every year.
I don't forget—I just like to keep the kids' photos authentic.

424. My kids asked why I take photos at drop-off.
Because I need evidence I was a responsible parent.

425. My mate asked why I avoid volunteering for the school fair.
Because I still have PTSD from the glitter station last year.

426. How do I explain history to my kids?
It's just old gossip that became important over time.

427. My wife asked why I always get picked for the raffle.
It's because I buy just enough tickets to look supportive but not desperate.

428. What's my tactic for remembering term dates?
Ask the school WhatsApp group and hope someone answers quickly.

429. My kids asked why I still pack apples for lunch.
Because it's the core of a balanced lunch!

430. My mate asked how I survived the school nativity play.

By clapping like every sheep deserved an Oscar.

431. What's my trick for calming first-day-of-school nerves?

I just tell them, "It'll only last 13 more years".

432. My wife asked why I'm bad at last-minute costume requests.

Bad? I think my bin-bag robot costume was a masterpiece!

433. My kids asked why I always say "back in my day".

Because it's the official phrase all dads use when they run out of arguments.

434. My mate asked why I still check for nits.

Because I like to stay 'ahead' of the problem.

435. What's my response to a surprise test result?

"Well done!"—followed by googling what the grade actually means.

436. My wife asked why I forgot school photo day again.

Why bother? It's not like they'll look at the camera anyway.

437. How do I react when helping my kid with their spelling?

I break into a cold sweat and start reciting the alphabet out loud—just in case.

438. My kids asked why I can't pronounce their school projects.

I can't pronounce them, but I bet I'll be the one building them.

439. My mate asked why I avoid school sports day races.

Because school sports day isn't ready for my world-class dad jog

440. What's my strategy for teacher appreciation gifts?

I like to add a personal note that says, "Thanks for surviving another year with my offspring".

441. My wife asked why I don't read the school newsletter.

I'm still waiting for the audiobook version narrated by the headteacher.

442. My kids asked why I never wave goodbye at drop-offs.

I tried once, but I accidentally hit the horn and scared everyone.

443. My mate asked how I handle school trips.

I just pretend I'm on holiday—minus the relaxation, cocktails, and fun.

444. What's my secret for surviving bake sales?

My secret? Never admitting which stall I bought my 'homemade' cake from.

445. My wife asked why the kids' lunch boxes are so basic.

Because the last time I got creative, it ended up looking like a food fight.

446. My kids asked why I call recess "break time".

Because recess is just too fancy a word for running in circles.

447. My kids asked why I still help with homework.

Because every time I help, I realise I'm learning more than you are!

448. My wife asked why I keep missing the school WhatsApp updates.

Oh, I'm sure the fate of the world depends on another cupcake sale update.

449. How do I explain modern geography to my kids?

It's all about where we live... and where we can't afford to visit.

450. My kids asked why I cheer the loudest at school plays.

Because it's the only time I get to yell in public without getting strange looks.

Congratulations, you've made it halfway through the parent-teacher conference of dad jokes! By now, you've mastered the art of packing lunches, faking enthusiasm for glitter-covered art projects, and Googling maths solutions while pretending to know the answer. The first 50 jokes were just the homework; now we're moving into the real test—field trips, parent races, and surviving the school WhatsApp group without losing your sanity. So grab your metaphorical red pen, take a deep breath, and let's tackle the second half like a spelling bee champion who just realised they're in the wrong room.

451. My kids asked why I always overpack for field trips.

"I like big *bags* and I cannot lie!"

452. How do I feel about the school WhatsApp group?

Like it's a never-ending conference call with no mute button.

453. My wife asked why I keep volunteering for chaperone duty.

Because I like wearing a high-vis jacket—three sizes too small.

454. What's my strategy for parent races on sports day?

I strategically position myself next to the dad who's wearing jeans.

455. My kids asked why I wear trainers to school events.

Because last year, I learned the hard way that you can't sprint in loafers

456. My mate asked how I handle glitter explosions from school art projects.

I treat glitter like snow—beautiful for five minutes, then a nightmare to clean up.

457. What's my favourite part of parent-teacher conferences?

The part where I accidentally sit on a tiny chair and get stuck.

458. My wife asked why I buy extra glue sticks.

Because you never know when there'll be a national glue stick shortage—better safe than sorry.

459. How do I handle costume day requests at the last minute?

I just *fabricate* something with whatever's lying around.

460. My kids asked why I always forget their packed lunch.
I'm teaching you survival skills!

461. My mate asked why I avoid the WhatsApp group debates.
Oh, I just *love* debating the colour of next year's school disco lights.

462. What's my reaction to "Dad, I need help with my essay"?
I start singing, "Another essay bites the dust!" while sharpening a pencil.

463. My wife asked why the kids' science project smells weird.
That might be my fault—I thought "add a bit of flair" meant garlic powder.

464. My kids asked why I cheer so much at sports day.
Because when I cheer loud enough, I swear it makes you run faster.

465. How do I survive field trips to museums?
I just pretend I'm part of the exhibit—stand still long enough and the kids move on.

466. My mate asked why I never win parent races.
Because I'm saving my energy for the post-race biscuit table.

467. What's my secret to handling school WhatsApp updates?
I've outsourced it to the cat—she seems as qualified as anyone else.

468. My kids asked why I always send them with extra pencils.

Because I know you'll lose one by first period, lend one by second, and chew the third by lunch.

469. My wife asked why I sign permission slips without reading them.

Because I trust the school to make sure they're only climbing reasonably *safe* mountains.

470. My mate asked how the school talent show went.

I clapped so hard my watch flew off and hit the headteacher— it got a standing ovation.

471. My kids asked why I love quiz night fundraisers.

Because nothing beats the thrill of arguing over which continent Madagascar belongs to.

472. How do I feel about school bake sales?

Bake sales are just competitions disguised as charity.

473. My wife asked why I buy ready-made cupcakes for bake sales.

Because I like the thrill of smuggling in Tesco's finest and calling them mine.

474. My mate asked why I avoid the playground after drop-off.

Last time, I stepped in a puddle, tripped over a scooter, and nearly landed in the sandpit.

475. How do I explain modern grammar homework to my kids?

I tell them it's like learning a secret code... for impressing their English teacher.

476. My wife asked why I leave sports kits drying on the radiator.
Because I can't figure out how to use the airing cupboard properly.

477. My kids asked why I hate book fairs.
Because they're a *novel* way to drain my wallet.

478. My kids asked why I always sit on the front row at school plays.
Because by the time I arrive, all the "safe" middle seats are already taken.

479. What's my favourite part of a school play?
Watching the kids wrestle with a backdrop that refuses to stay in place.

480. My wife asked why I keep losing school newsletters.
Obviously, I treasure every single newsletter so much that I've hidden them somewhere even I can't find

481. How do I handle the costume competition?
By reminding myself that this is about 'creativity' and not who spends the most on Amazon Prime.

482. My wife asked why I keep buying school raffle tickets.
Clearly, I can't resist the 'once-in-a-lifetime' chance to win a bottle of cheap wine.

483. My kids asked why I always carry tissues to school events.

Because last time, I sneezed mid-applause and needed a tissue for the row in front of me.

484. My wife asked why the school WhatsApp group annoys me.

Because the conversations are so riveting—who doesn't love a three-hour argument about joggers?

485. How do I survive a trip to the school carnival?

I treat it like a tactical mission: avoid the stalls with glitter, target the ones with cake.

486. My kids asked why I never remember to pack raincoats.

I hum, 'Raindrops keep falling on your head,' as I search for the coats I forgot to pack.

487. My mate asked why I struggle with sports day logistics.

Because I can't *field* all the demands thrown my way.

488. My wife asked how I managed to forget non-uniform day again.

Because I clearly have a *uniform approach* to forgetting things.

489. My kids asked why I never get the maths questions right.

"These questions are written by someone who clearly hates parents".

490. My mate asked how I prepare for a school disco.

By treating the disco like the Hunger Games—survival is the ultimate goal.

491. My wife asked why I struggle with homework time.

Because the one time I'm confident in an answer, my kid says, "That's not how Miss does it."

492. My kids asked why I don't know modern geography.

Because when I went to school, half the countries on today's map didn't even exist.

493. My mate asked why I bring snacks to sports day.

Because snacks are the secret to staying calm when your kid drops the baton again.

494. My wife asked why I never join the PTA.

Last time I attended a meeting, I accidentally volunteered to organise the summer fair while sneezing.

495. My kids asked why I clap too loudly at school plays.

Because someone has to fill the awkward silence after the tambourine solo.

496. My kids teacher asked why I'm late to drop-off.

I got the kids in the car and realised I was still in my slippers.

497. How do I survive bake sales?

By buying just enough cookies to avoid being 'that parent'.

498. My wife asked why I keep missing the school calendar updates.

Because my notifications are drowned in WhatsApp chaos.

499. My kids asked why I make the same sandwich every day.

Because creativity is for after school, not before coffee.

500. My mate asked how I survive parent races.
I stay focused on the finish line—and not the crowd laughing at my technique.

The 50% Mark: Dads Don't Quit

You did it! You've officially made it halfway through this epic journey of dadhood, dad jokes, and dad struggles. From surviving *Parenting Perils*—where we learned that bedtime is less of a routine and more of a tactical battle—to mastering the mysterious world of *Money Matters* (and probably starting a new spreadsheet). You've tackled the *Tech Troubles*, wrestled with smartphones, and still somehow avoided turning your Wi-Fi router into a frisbee. But you didn't stop there. No, you took on *DIY Disasters* like a seasoned pro, and let's be honest: if anyone asks about the crooked shelves, just tell them it's 'artistic flair'.

Then came *School Days*, where you ventured into the land of parent-teacher meetings, art projects that could double as glitter bombs, and somehow managing to forget yet another picture day. You showed up for every field trip, packed lunch, and mandatory school event—often in mismatched socks and with the distinct look of a dad who's survived a 10-hour meeting and just wants a nap.

And now here we are, at the *50% Mark: Dads Don't Quit*, where your ability to make it through the first half of this book is a testament to your resilience. Sure, you've still got *Fitness Fiascos* to navigate, but you've already built up the stamina for the next round. Whether it's dodging leg day or trying to remember what 'muscle memory' means, you've been through it all and are still standing—probably with snacks in hand.

As we dive into Office Antics, you've already endured your share of awkward small talk, last-minute deadlines, and endless email chains. But don't worry, the real office chaos is just getting started. From dodging team-building exercises to surviving another round of "just one quick meeting," you'll navigate every workday curveball with the determination of a Dad who knows quitting isn't an option—especially when there's free coffee involved.

Looking ahead, we've also got *Sports Shenanigans* waiting for you. Get ready to channel your inner coach and cheer on your team, whether they're actually winning or just out there for the snacks. *Car Catastrophes* will test your ability to stay calm during breakdowns and mysterious engine noises, and *Shopping Struggles* will challenge your skills at navigating the aisles and figuring out what 'on sale' really means. You've survived the first half; now it's time to power through the second.

And don't forget, the grand finale is just around the corner. The 1001st Dad Joke awaits, and it's going to be the crowning moment of this journey. But no need to worry—by the time we get there, you'll have earned your dad-joke supremacy with every misstep, every laugh, and every lesson along the way.

So, let's keep going, because the second half of this journey promises even more hilarious mishaps, dad victories, and all the dad moments you've been waiting for. The best is yet to come, and we're only just getting started!

Fitness Fiascos

Fitness. The word alone is enough to make some dads break a sweat—even if they're just sitting down. We all have that one exercise routine that sounds good in theory: a few laps around the block, a few sets of weights, and maybe—just maybe—actually sticking to it. But in reality? It's more about surviving the warm-up, figuring out how to use all that strange gym equipment, and convincing ourselves that a walk to the fridge counts as cardio.

This chapter is dedicated to every Dad who's ever bought a set of dumbbells and then used them to hold the door open, or tried yoga only to discover their flexibility has gone AWOL. From pretending to stretch to sprinting in slow motion, these jokes prove that the journey to fitness is full of laughs—and sometimes, it's more about laughing than lifting. Whether it's signing up for a gym membership with great intentions only to quit before you've even used the locker room, or getting tangled in resistance bands like they're a high-tech form of rope, we've all been there. Fitness isn't just a goal—it's a series of hilarious attempts at being healthier that somehow end with a snack and a nap.

501. How do I stay motivated to work out?
By putting on gym clothes and calling it 'preparation'.

502. My wife asked why I always use the treadmill as a clothes rack.
Because it gets lonely.

503. How do I handle a yoga class?
By pretending I know what downward dog is and hoping no one notices.

504. My kids asked why I can't do a pull-up.
I'm waiting for my muscles to make a grand entrance.

505. What's my favourite type of workout?
The one that involves sitting down and eating pizza.

506. My wife asked why I bought another gym membership.
Because they gave me a free water bottle.

507. How do I get in my steps?
I outsource them to my smart watch. It's the real fitness guru.

508. My kids asked why I call it 'muscle memory'.
Because my muscles remember how to avoid exercise.

509. Why do I never use the rowing machine?
Because it keeps asking me for a boarding pass.

510. My wife asked why I keep saying I'm 'too tired' to work out.

Because my body's primary function is to nap.

511. How do I survive a run?
By running just far enough to convince myself I deserve a medal—and a doughnut.

512. My kids asked why I never finish my home workouts.
Because every time I try, my body sends an error message.

513. What's my strategy for a healthy breakfast?
It's simple: I stare at the fruit bowl, then eat a muffin instead.

514. My mate asked why I keep buying gym clothes.
Because they make me look like someone who works out, even if I never do.

515. Why do I avoid leg day?
Because I don't like explaining to strangers why I'm walking like a baby giraffe.

516. My wife asked why I never do squats.
Because squats are just elaborate sitting—and I prefer the simpler version.

517. How do I prepare for a run?
By spending 20 minutes choosing the perfect playlist... for a 10-minute run.

518. My kids asked why I'm always breathing heavily after a jog.
Because I'm built for comfort, not cardio.

519. Why do I always choose the elliptical over the treadmill?
Because it's a 'fancy' way of walking, and I like to feel sophisticated.

520. My wife asked why I never finish my 5K.
Because I'm more of a '5-minute' kind of guy.

521. How do I approach new workout routines?
By watching a YouTube video and pretending I can follow along.

522. My mate asked why I never use the punching bag.
Because I'm more of a 'punching air in frustration' kind of guy.

523. What's my excuse for not going to the gym?
I'm on a groundbreaking fitness program called 'Netflix and Stretch.' It's revolutionary.

524. My wife asked why I only go to the gym once a month.
Once a month keeps my gym membership alive and my excuses thriving.

525. How do I deal with sore muscles?
I convince myself it's a sign of progress while crying softly into an ice pack.

526. My kids asked why I look so stiff after a workout.
This is what peak athleticism looks like—don't let anyone tell you otherwise.

527. Why do I avoid the weightlifting section at the gym?

I'm just giving the pros some space to shine—consider it a public service.

528. My wife asked why I need so many gym towels.

Because I use them as 'mood blankets' to remind myself that I tried.

529. How do I prepare for a family hike?

By pretending to be excited while secretly hoping for a shortcut back to the car.

530. My mate asked why I always choose walking over running.

Have you ever seen anyone look happy while running? Neither have I.

531. What's my favourite post-workout snack?

A whole pizza. It's balanced, right?

532. My kids asked why I never finish my yoga poses.

Because I'm 'resting' my way to flexibility.

533. How do I track my fitness progress?

I check if I can bend down to tie my shoes—without needing a recovery nap.

534. My wife asked why I never finish a home workout video.

I'm saving the second half of the workout for my next year's resolutions.

535. What's my excuse for not using the bike at the gym?
I'm waiting for them to add a motor—until then, I'm out.

536. My mate asked why I never stretch before working out.
Because stretching before a workout feels like studying before a pop quiz—pointless.

537. How do I handle my first day at the gym?
By pretending I know how to use every machine, then pretending I'm injured when I can't.

538. My wife asked why I always choose cardio machines with screens.
Because if I can't be entertained, I'll just fall asleep.

539. What's my strategy for weight loss?
I call it the 'See Food Diet'—I see food, I eat it.

540. My mate asked why I haven't lost weight.
Because I'm in a committed relationship... with carbs.

541. How do I survive a workout class?
By pretending I'm just warming up when I'm actually near death.

542. My wife asked why I always sit down after a run.
Because if I don't sit, I might fall.

543. What's my excuse for not using the rowing machine?
I prefer my boats to have a captain.

544. My kids asked why I always skip burpees.

Because there's a rule in the Dad fitness manual: avoid all movements that involve the floor.

545. How do I keep motivated to run?

I imagine there's a pizza waiting at the finish line.

546. My mate asked why I don't do crunches.

Because my abs are perfectly hidden under this dad bod.

547. What's my solution to bad posture?

By blaming it on 'bad office chairs' and 'too many Netflix marathons'.

548. My wife asked why I don't use the stair climber.

Because stairs are already a punishment at home—no need to simulate them.

549. How do I avoid embarrassing gym moments?

By going during 'quiet hours' and praying I don't make eye contact with anyone.

550. My kids asked why I wear gym clothes outside the house.

I'm testing their durability—so far, they've survived three brunches.

Well done! You've made it halfway through this fitness fiasco, and at this point, if you're not sore, you're probably not doing it right—or you've accidentally taken a nap halfway through your workout. This is the part where the sweat begins to feel more like regret, and that post-workout glow turns into a desperate search for the nearest chair to collapse into. But fear not— every stretch, every groan, every "I'm just warming up" is a victory, even if the only thing getting stronger is your resolve to never work out again. So, grab a protein shake (or, you know, a doughnut) and let's get back into it. The second half of this chapter is all about pushing through, even when you're convinced your muscles are staging a revolt.

551. My kids asked why I'm always out of breath after a walk.
Because 'cardio' and I have a complicated relationship.

552. What's my excuse for not lifting heavier weights?
Hey, my muscles are still in development... and so is my motivation.

553. My wife asked why I always complain after doing squats.
Complaining is how I burn the extra calories..

554. How do I know I've pushed myself too hard at the gym?
When my muscles start sending me "Please stop" messages.

555. My mate asked why I never join him for a run.
Because I'm still recovering from the last time I sprinted for the bus.

556. What's my fitness philosophy?
"Go hard or go home"—I prefer home.

557. My wife asked why I never stretch before a workout.

I skip the stretch so I can focus on the important stuff—like avoiding the gym altogether.

558. How do I handle a marathon workout session?
By taking a break every 2 minutes to 'reassess' my life choices.

559. My kids asked why I'm always holding my back after lifting.
I'm giving it moral support—it's been through a lot today.

560. What's my plan for a full-body workout?
Start with push-ups, switch to planks, then finish strong by collapsing dramatically.

561. My mate asked why I don't do yoga.
Because 'bending like a pretzel' sounds like something for someone else.

562. How do I feel after doing push-ups?
Like I just fought a war with the floor—and the floor won.

563. My wife asked why I only go to the gym once a week.
Because the gym and I are in a long-distance relationship.

564. What's my trick for staying in shape?
Move from the couch to the fridge as quickly as possible.

565. My kids asked why I always take the elevator instead of the stairs.
Stairs want you to prove something—elevators just accept you as you are.

566. How do I track my workout progress?

By counting how many snacks I can eat after I've 'burned some calories'.

567. My mate asked why I never join him for cycling.

I prefer my vehicles with engines and air conditioning.

568. Why do I call skipping leg day 'strategic planning'?

Because if I never use my legs, they'll last longer—simple math.

569. How do I stay fit without hitting the gym?

I chase my kids around the house; it's a high-intensity interval workout.

570. My wife asked why I'm always so sore after working out.

Because my muscles didn't sign up for this, and they're letting me know it.

571. What's my idea of a great workout?

Anything that doesn't involve sweat... or effort.

572. My mate asked how I survive the elliptical machine.

By setting it to 'low resistance' and pretending it's a roller-coaster.

573. Why do I always buy new gym clothes?

Because if I'm going to fail at working out, I at least want to look good doing it.

574. My kids asked why I always make them go for walks.

Because every family walk is practice for when you have to push me in a wheelchair someday.

575. What's my approach to fitness classes?

Avoid eye contact with the instructor and hope they don't call me out.

576. My wife asked why I don't like running.

Because running away from responsibility is already exhausting enough.

577. How do I feel after a workout?

Like a champion... until I sit down and can't get back up.

578. My mate asked why I don't use the pull-down machine.

Last time I tried it, I nearly launched myself into orbit.

579. Why do I avoid the gym's heavy weights section?

The weights and I have a deal: I don't touch them, and they don't embarrass me.

580. My kids asked why I never go to spin class.

The only spinning I like involves chairs.

581. What's my approach to weight loss?

My plan is simple: eat healthy Monday to Friday, then let chaos reign on the weekends.

582. My wife asked why I only do 'low-impact' exercises.

It's not low-impact; it's 'responsible fitness'.

583. How do I survive my fitness tracker?

By ignoring it when it says 'Move!'—I'm not taking orders from a watch.

584. My mate asked why I don't try a personal trainer.

Because if I wanted someone to tell me I'm doing it wrong, I'd just ask my wife.

585. Why do I feel like a champion after a 5-minute workout?

Because I've been in denial for the other 55 minutes.

586. My wife asked why I'm always sore after doing the dishes.

Because lifting the plates feels like lifting weights at this point.

587. What's my go-to workout routine?

I call it the 'One Set Wonder'—one set, and I'm done.

588. My mate asked why I only do yoga at home.

Because I can collapse in private without being judged.

589. Why do I never track my steps?

My steps are private—it's between me and my sofa.

590. My wife asked why I hate stretching.

Because every time I stretch, I can hear my legs are whispering, "Why are you doing this to us?"

591. How do I deal with gym memberships?

Like a donation—I give generously and visit rarely.

592. My kids asked why I never join them for a game of tag.
Tag is just cardio in disguise, and I'm not falling for it.

593. What's my idea of a great fitness challenge?
Trying to open a jar of pickles.

594. My wife asked why I never finish my 10-minute workout videos.
Because after 3 minutes, I'm already on the floor in a 'resting' position.

595. How do I handle running on the treadmill?
By staring at the timer like it owes me an apology.

596. My mate asked why I never take gym selfies.
No filter can make 'sweaty and confused' look good.

597. Why do I avoid fitness classes?
Because I'm just here for the free water and the uncomfortable stretching.

598. My wife asked why I keep *talking* about getting fit.
I'm just trying to convince myself it's a good idea—so far, no luck.

599. What's my secret to fitness motivation?
I tell myself I'm just one workout away from looking like an action star.

600. My kids asked why I'm always so tired after the gym.
Because my body isn't built for fitness—it's built for snacks.

Office Antics

Office Antics: Every Dad knows that the office is the prime location for questionable jokes, harmless pranks, and a whole lot of "did I really just say that?" moments. Whether it's cracking the same old "Is it Friday yet?" line or attempting to navigate the chaos of Zoom meetings, Dads bring a unique sense of humour to the workday.

This chapter dives into the hilarity of office antics—awkward small talk by the water cooler, impromptu attempts at "motivational" emails, and the art of pretending to understand jargon during conference calls. So grab your mug, put on your best office-appropriate grin, and let's laugh through the daily grind.

601. My boss asked why I always bring in a giant coffee mug.

Because regular mugs can't handle my caffeine needs—or my emotional baggage

602. How do I survive a meeting with my manager?

By reminding myself that no one knows what's going on—especially the manager.

603. My colleague asked why I always sit by the window in the office.

I like to keep one eye on my escape route.

604. Why do I keep a stress ball on my desk?

Because I need something to squeeze that won't file an HR complaint.

605. My head of department asked why I'm always the first to leave the office.

Because I like to leave while I still have a shred of sanity left.

606. How do I deal with conference calls?

By muting my mic and hoping no one notices my dramatic eye roll.

607. My colleague asked why I'm always wearing a blazer to Zoom meetings.

Because it's the only way I can look professional while wearing sweatpants.

608. What's my go-to strategy when HR sends out a new policy?

I save it to a folder titled "Things I'll Never Open".

609. Why do I always bring snacks to work?

Because it's the "snackrifice" I make to survive the day.

610. How do I know when it's time to leave the office?

When the office plants begin whispering, "Run while you can".

611. My manager asked why I'm always the last to sign off on a project.

Because I'm convinced the slower I finish, the less likely I'll be asked to do it again.

612. What's my tactic for surviving office gossip?

I laugh nervously and hope no one brings up my name.

613. My colleague asked why I always bring in my own lunch.

Because nothing says "success" like Tupperware from three years ago.

614. Why do I love team-building exercises?

Because bonding over how much we hate team-building is the ultimate team-builder.

615. How do I handle my boss's vague instructions?

I nod and say, "Got it!" while internally screaming.

616. My HR manager asked why I'm always so calm in high-stress situations.

Because deep down, I know that no one else knows what they're doing either.

617. Why do I always take a long lunch break?

Because I need extra time to convince myself to go back to work.

618. How do I survive awkward office parties?

By saying, "This is fun!" repeatedly until someone lets me leave.

619. My boss asked why I always look so busy.

Because if I look busy enough, no one questions what I'm actually doing.

620. What's my trick for surviving a presentation?

I make eye contact with the one person who looks just as confused as me.

621. How do I prepare for a Zoom meeting with the big boss?

I triple-check my camera angle to make sure no one sees my pyjama bottoms.

622. My colleague asked why I always respond to emails with a joke.

Because humour distracts from the fact that I have no real answers.

623. Why do I always look confused in meetings?

Because I'm trying to figure out if anyone else understands what's happening.

624. How do I deal with the office printer?

I casually walk away as if I wasn't the one who caused the paper jam.

625. Why do I always answer "no" when asked if I'm available for another meeting?

Because I thrive on missing meetings that should've been emails.

626. My boss asked why I always have a spare pen on my desk.

Because the last time I didn't, I spent 15 minutes pretending to take notes with a broken highlighter.

627. How do I know when it's Friday?
When I suddenly develop a very convincing "out of office" email response.

628. Why do I always bring my own coffee to work?
Because I don't trust the office kettle—it looks like it's been through a war.

629. How do I survive Monday mornings?
By reminding myself that the weekend is only five days away.

630. My colleague asked why I'm always on the phone.
Because pretending to be busy is an art form, and I'm a master.

631. Why do I never volunteer for office committees?
Because I imagine every committee meeting as a black hole where time disappears forever.

632. How do I handle workplace criticism?
By nodding thoughtfully and then sending passive-aggressive emails later.

633. Why do I always carry a notebook?
I like to pretend it's filled with groundbreaking ideas—when really, it's doodles.

634. What's my go-to excuse for being late to work?
I got caught up in a philosophical debate—with my toaster.

635. Why do I always avoid talking to HR?

I'm convinced they're keeping a secret file on how many times I've googled "how to look busy".

636. How do I know when my workday is truly over?

When I start debating whether my stapler is worth stealing.

637. Why do I have a thousand sticky notes on my desk?

Because I'm secretly building a fortress of procrastination.

638. My colleague asked why I'm always so prepared for meetings.

Because I've got an entire "I have no idea what's going on" script rehearsed.

639. How do I deal with office politics?

I masterfully agree with both sides, even when they're in the same room.

640. Why do I always have a backup charger at work?

Because if my phone dies, how else will I check memes during meetings?

641. My boss asked why I never volunteer to take minutes in meetings?

Because I can't summarise my own thoughts, let alone an entire meeting.

642. How do I approach a pay rise with my boss.

I start with: "I'm here to talk about the one thing more important than work: my paycheck."

643. How do I handle surprise deadlines?

By smiling and saying, "Sure, no problem! I'm happy to drop everything".

644. Why do I always volunteer for coffee runs?

Because I enjoy pretending to be a responsible adult while I'm actually avoiding the real work.

645. My boss asked why I always email so early in the morning.

Because scheduling emails for 7am makes me look like a hardworking genius.

646. How do I prepare for performance reviews?

By practising saying "I'll work on that" in the mirror with a straight face.

647. My manager asked why I never laugh at their jokes.

Because I'm on a strict "only laugh when it's absolutely necessary" diet.

648. Why do I always avoid sitting in the front row at presentations?

Because I like to keep a safe distance from anyone holding a laser pointer.

649. My colleague asked why I bring noise-cancelling headphones to work.

Because when Karen from HR starts another story about her weekend, it's time to hit the 'mute' button.

650. How do I survive office birthday celebrations?

By clapping awkwardly and pretending I didn't forget to sign the card.

Congratulations! You've made it through the first half of the office antics, and by now, you've probably perfected your "I'm totally paying attention" face during meetings. This is where the real fun begins: the awkward small talk by the water cooler, the last-minute deadlines that come with zero instructions, and the boss's motivational speeches that somehow leave you more confused than inspired. By now, you've mastered the art of looking busy while mentally planning your lunch. So, grab your coffee mug, brace yourself for the next round of office emails, and let's keep laughing through the daily grind.

651. My colleague asked why I always send emails at odd hours.

Because I like to keep everyone guessing whether I'm a night owl or just completely unhinged.

652. How do I handle the office fridge wars?

By labelling my lunch with "HR experiment" to keep everyone away.

653. My boss asked why I never answer calls on my lunch break.

I'm too busy trying to chew on my food and my life choices at the same time.

654. Why do I always avoid the break room at 10am?

Because it's where the 'motivational' posters live, and I can't handle that much positivity before coffee.

655. How do I survive the weekly team check-ins?

By using phrases like "good progress" and hoping no one asks for specifics.

656. My colleague asked why I always bring a blanket to work.

Because I'm convinced my desk is secretly located in the North Pole.

657. Why do I always take the longest route to my desk?

Because I'm avoiding the one colleague who *always* wants to talk about their weekend.

658. My boss asked why I'm always the first to leave team-building activities.

Because 'team-building' feels a lot like 'mandatory social torture' to me.

659. How do I survive the quarterly review?

By pretending I understand the graphs while secretly wondering if they're upside down.

660. My colleague asked why I always have a backup USB drive.

Because I don't like taking chances—I prefer to 'stick' to safety.

661. Why do I keep my desk so tidy?

Because it distracts from the chaos happening inside my inbox.

662. My manager asked why I'm always the first to volunteer for presentations.
Because if I go first, I don't have to sit through anyone else's.

663. How do I prepare for office fire drills?
By treating it like a real emergency, which means grabbing my coffee first.

664. Why do I always print extra copies for meetings?
Because you never know when a spontaneous origami demonstration might break out.

665. My colleague asked why I always bring a reusable water bottle to work.
Because it's the only bottle I can bring to work without HR getting involved.

666. Why do I always agree to 'catch-up' chats with my boss?
Because nothing says 'I'm interested' like nodding along while wondering how soon it will end.

667. How do I survive working late on a Friday?
By pretending I don't have any social plans, which, to be fair, is mostly true.

668. Why do I always avoid eye contact during meetings?
Because I'm afraid they'll see the panic in my eyes when I have no idea what's going on.

669. Why do I keep a plant on my desk?

It helps me 'branch' out from all the negativity around here.

670. My manager asked why I always avoid making Power-Points.

Because I believe in the ancient art of interpretive hand gestures.

671. How do I dress for casual Fridays?

By trying to find the sweet spot between 'fashionably casual' and 'getting an HR email'.

672. My colleague asked why I never join after-work drinks.

Because I prefer my stress relief to be quiet—and not surrounded by the people who caused it.

673. Why do I keep a pack of biscuits in my drawer?

Because bribing my way out of extra work is a solid strategy.

674. My boss asked why I never double-check my emails.

Because I find that people pay more attention when they're trying to decipher what I meant.

675. How do I handle office arguments?

By breaking out the popcorn and asking if anyone else needs a drink before it gets really good.

676. My colleague asked why I always bring my own keyboard to work.

Because the office keyboards are so sticky that sometimes I feel like I'm trying to pry open a bank vault.

677. Why do I never write down questions during meetings?

Because my only question I have is "When will this end?" and I don't need to write that down.

678. My manager asked why I always sit at the back during presentations.

Because I like being near the exit in case things get 'interactive'.

679. How do I survive the annual office Christmas party?

By pretending I'm allergic to karaoke and secret Santa exchanges.

680. My colleague asked why I never delete old emails.

Because one day, my 'Sent Items' folder will be my memoir.

681. Why do I always keep an extra pair of shoes under my desk?

It's my version of 'office survival gear'—along with extra coffee and a fake smile.

682. Why do I never use the office microwave?

Because I've seen things go into that microwave that I'm pretty sure void the laws humanity.

683. How do I prepare for office presentations?

By memorising the phrase "Let's circle back to that."

684. My colleague asked why I always have a coffee cup in hand.

Because it's the only thing that prevents me from gesturing

wildly during meetings.

685. Why do I avoid 'open-door policies'?

Because the door may be open, but my interest in walking through it is definitely closed.

686. My manager asked why I always carry sticky notes.

Because they're the closest thing I have to a personal assistant.

687. What's my go-to for the office shared-lunch?

Anything I can 'dish out' without anyone suspecting it's from the reduced section.

688. My colleague asked why I always book the smallest meeting room.

Because nothing builds team spirit like the threat of running out of oxygen.

689. Why do I always join video calls with my camera off?

Because I like to spare everyone the sight of my 'work-from-home fashion choices'—which are mostly pyjamas.

690. My boss asked why I always reply "Sounds good" to meeting invites.

Because it sounds better than "I have no choice".

691. Why do I keep emergency chocolate in my drawer?

Because it's either emergency chocolate or emergency tears.

692. My manager asked why I always write in pencil.

I like the option to erase my ideas before anyone realizes how bad they were.

693. How do I survive performance evaluations?

By auto responding to every comment with "That's a great point".

694. My colleague asked why I always send gifs in emails.

Because a looping clip of a hamster spinning out of control is the best metaphor for office life.

695. Why do I avoid office stand ups?

Nothing says 'productive morning' like awkwardly summarizing my lack of progress in front of everyone.

696. My manager asked why I always call IT for help.

Because I can never remember I need to switch it 'on and off' again, or the other way around.

697. What's my approach to shared workspaces?

To occupy just enough space to look productive, while secretly hoping no one notices I've been staring at the same spreadsheet for hours.

698. My boss asked why I never include pie charts in presentations.

Because no one takes me seriously when I compare our quarterly losses to slices of dessert.

699. Why do I always respond "Interesting" during brainstorming sessions?

It's vague enough to sound supportive, but non-committal enough to dodge blame if it goes wrong.

700. My colleague asked why I always decline calendar invites.

Because I believe meetings are like vampires—if you don't invite them in, they can't drain the life out of you.

Sports Shenanigans

Sports—the universal stage where Dads shine brightest, even if only in their own minds. Whether we're recounting our 'glory days' with just a hint of exaggeration or passionately coaching from the couch, sports give us endless opportunities for both triumph and hilarity.

This chapter celebrates the Dads who run out of breath after one lap but claim it's "just the warm-up". From backyard games to questionable refereeing calls, these jokes prove that while Dads may not always score, we definitely bring our A-game to the comedy field.

701. My kids asked why I always yell at the TV during sports.
Because I'm coaching them... they just don't know it yet.

702. How do I handle watching sports with my kids?
By explaining the rules in terms they can understand: "Just like when you argue about who gets the last cookie".

703. My wife asked why I'm so competitive with the kids.
Because every time I win, it's another victory for the *dad*

legacy.

704. Why do I refuse to let the kids win at board games?

Because if they can't handle a little competition now, they'll never survive family game night.

705. My mate asked why I always claim to have been an "athlete" in my youth.

Because "athlete" sounds better than "guy who got winded playing dodgeball".

706. How do I motivate my kids during a soccer game?

By yelling "You're doing great!"—even if they've been running in the wrong direction for five minutes.

707. My kids asked why I always say, "Back in my day..."

Because 'back in my day', I was the undefeated champion of eating sweets before dinner without getting caught.

708. Why do I still think I can win a race with the kids?

Because my ego insists that winning against a child is a victory worth pursuing.

709. My wife asked why I'm always 'coaching' the kids from the sidelines.

I like to imagine myself as a retired professional giving back—even if it's just to a Under 7's football game.

710. How do I survive a family sports game?

By conveniently 'forgetting' the rules whenever I'm losing

711. My kids asked why I always say "I used to be faster".

Because the truth is too painful—especially when I see them sprint past me.

712. Why do I get so excited when I win at family sports?

Because it's the only chance I get to show the kids how it's done.

713. My mate asked why I always argue with the referee.

Because every call feels like a personal attack on my 'extensive knowledge' of the game.

714. What's my tactic for winning at backyard games?

I make up new rules as I go along—hey, it's my game!

715. My wife asked why I'm always the loudest one at sports events.

Because my athletic skills are long gone, but my vocal cords are still in prime condition.

716. How do I know when I've had enough of a sports game?

When I'm ready to trade all my enthusiasm for a hot dog and a quiet corner.

717. My kids asked why I'm always talking about my 'sports career'.

Because in my mind, I'm still a legend in the making.

718. What's my strategy for coaching the kids' soccer game?

Shout words of wisdom like "Just kick it!"—works every time.

719. Why do I always play referee when we play sports as a family?

Because in my mind, I'm an elite official—complete with imaginary VAR technology.

720. My wife asked why I always try to coach the kids' games from the sidelines.

Because, in my head, I'm a professional coach with years of experience... and zero qualifications.

721. How do I deal with losing a game?

By saying, "It's not about winning or losing, it's about playing with heart"—then sulking in silence for a while.

722. My kids asked why I always insist on playing 'the best position'.

Because in my mind, I'm still the star player, even if I'm just standing in goal.

723. What's my approach to family sports?

I make sure to bring all the gear, even if no one else wants to play.

724. My mate asked why I get so worked up over the kids' sporting events.

Because there's something poetic about losing my mind over a game where no one is keeping score except for the parents.

725. How do I keep the kids entertained during a game?

By inventing new, completely made-up sports, like 'backyard dodgeball meets hopscotch'.

726. My wife asked why I always pretend to be tired after playing sports.

Because if I pretend I'm exhausted, I get to take a break while everyone else keeps playing.

727. Why do I act like I'm still an athlete?

Because every time I lift groceries, I imagine it's my Olympic weightlifting moment—minus the audience and the gold medal.

728. My kids asked why I always try to turn every game into a competition.

Because if you're not sweating and trash-talking during game of catch, what are you even playing it for?

729. How do I make sports more fun for the kids?

By giving everyone code names like 'Speedy' or 'The Wall'—of course, I'm 'The Bench Warmer'.

730. My wife asked why I always claim to be 'better' at every sport.

I'm just trying to keep my 'record' intact—even if that record is mostly made up.

731. Why do I always talk about my 'glory days'?

Because my highlight reel is a masterpiece of exaggeration and selective memory.

732. My wife asked why I always bring up my old sports achievements.

Because those old glory days are all I've got now—unless folding laundry becomes an Olympic event.

733. What's my secret to family sports games?

Make the rules vague enough so that I can still win, no matter what happens.

734. How do I handle the pressure of refereeing?

By making sure I give myself all the penalties.

735. My kids asked why I always volunteer to go in goal.

Oh, I don't know—maybe because I love standing still while dodging incoming shots aimed directly at my face?

736. Why do I love family sports events?

Because nothing beats watching Aunt Carol try to kick a soccer ball and ending up on her backside instead.

737. My mate asked why I make such a big deal about winning at sports.

Because 'winning' is the only thing I've got left to brag about!

738. How do I celebrate a sports victory?

By pretending it was a team effort while I internally gloat for hours.

739. My kids asked why I always use the "good old days" as an excuse for why I can't play anymore.

Because "good old days" sounds way better than "I'm out of shape".

740. Why do I always bring up my high school sports career?

Because it's a legacy that I've carefully crafted in my mind, and I'm sticking to it.

741. My wife asked why I always say "Just one more game!"
Because deep down, I'm hoping I'll suddenly get better at it.

742. How do I handle being the least athletic dad?
By wearing the coolest gear and acting like it's the outfit, not the ability, that makes the athlete.

743. My mate asked why I insist on being the team captain.
Because let's be honest—being the captain is mostly about flipping the coin at the start, and I'm really good at that.

744. How do I take a loss?
I re-enact my dramatic 'fall to the ground in despair'—it's my signature move.

745. My kids asked why I keep challenging them to races.
Because I enjoy the feeling of being completely out of breath and regretting all my life choices.

746. How do I motivate my kids to win?
By promising them that if they win, we'll hold a parade... down our street, with the neighbour's dog as the grand marshal.

747. My wife asked why I always think I'm still in shape.
Because round is a shape.

748. Why do I claim to be the best at sports?
Because dad ego is powerful—and sometimes, delusional.

749. My kids asked why I keep making up random sports rules.
Because every good game needs a referee with absolutely no

clue what they're doing—consider me that guy.

750. How do I feel after a sports game?

Like I need a medal for surviving it—and a nap.

Well done, champ! You've made it halfway through the *Sports Shenanigans* chapter, and let's be honest, you've probably worked up a sweat just reading this far. At this point, if you're not out of breath, you're either a superhero or you've found a cosy spot on the couch, pretending you're 'just resting' before the next big game. Whether you've been pretending to coach your kids from the sidelines, using your 'glory days' to boost your confidence, or inventing your own rules just to ensure a win, you've shown that being a dad in the sporting world is less about the game and more about the entertainment value. But don't get too comfortable—there's still plenty more sports-related shenanigans ahead. Grab your whistle, stretch those legs (or not), and let's dive back in. The second half is bound to be a whole new level of dad-athlete chaos!

751. My kids asked why I always say I used to be 'fast'.

Because if I say it enough, maybe I'll believe it too.

752. How do I make family sports more fun?

By pretending I'm a sports commentator narrating every play, complete with wildly exaggerated descriptions of my own 'heroic' contributions.

753. My wife asked why I always argue with other parents on

the sidelines.

Because nothing says 'good sportsmanship' like arguing over a game that's supposed to be all about the kids having fun.

754. Why do I insist on being the team captain?

It gives me a chance to show off my 'leadership' skills, even if those skills mostly involve pointing and shouting.

755. My mate asked why I make such a big deal about 'winning'.

I like to think of myself as the Michael Jordan of dad sports— except, you know, without the talent, fame, or endorsements.

756. What's my excuse for losing at sports?

I spent all my energy on the pep talk at the beginning.

757. My kids asked why I think I'm a sports expert.

Because explaining the rules incorrectly is my superpower.

758. How do I survive a kids' soccer game?

By shouting random motivational quotes that sound good but have no relevance to the game.

759. My wife asked why I always claim to have been a 'star athlete' in high school.

Because if I keep saying it, I'm hoping one day the universe will rewrite history and make it true.

760. Why do I always argue with the referee?

Because clearly, all my years of watching sports from the couch make me more qualified than someone with actual referee credentials.

761. My kids asked why I'm always the loudest one at a game.
Because I believe that, deep down, the referee needs my guidance, and I'm just trying to be helpful.

762. How do I handle a loss?
I declare it was 'just practice' and stop off into the changing room.

763. My mate asked why I always volunteer to referee.
Because if I can't win, at least I can control the game.

764. Why do I never let the kids win?
Because giving them a win would make too much sense, and I'm not here for that.

765. My wife asked why I always act like I'm in 'game mode'.
Because I need to make sure I'm ready for all possible scenarios—like when the neighbour's dog joins our soccer game unexpectedly.

766. How do I know I'm winning at family sports?
Because I'm the one 'calling the shots'—and also, the one who gets to choose when the game ends.

767. My kids asked why I'm always trying to set up 'training sessions'.
Because the Olympics are just around the corner, and I want us all to be ready... for the backyard version.

768. What's my secret to winning backyard games?

Bribing the referee... who just so happens to be me. It's a flawless system.

769. My wife asked why I always try to coach during family games.

Because nothing says 'relaxed family fun' quite like Dad turning every game into a strategic masterclass.

770. How do I deal with my competitive spirit?

I just 'play it cool'—by pretending I'm not keeping score, even when I totally am.

771. My kids asked why I always challenge them to races.

Because nothing says 'athletic prowess' quite like being left in the dust by a couple of kids under 10.

772. Why do I still think I'm the fastest runner in the family?

Because denial is a very powerful motivator.

773. My wife asked why I never let the kids pick the teams.

Because I like to keep things 'fair and square'—which, coincidentally, always means me ending up with the strongest players

774. How do I get the kids to play sports?

By telling them that if they score enough goals, they might unlock 'Dad's Secret Ice Cream Stash'—which may or may not actually exist.

775. My wife asked why I always challenge the kids to 'friendly'

competitions.

Because nothing says 'friendly' quite like Dad diving across the lawn to prevent losing at tug-of-war.

776. What's my trick for getting out of sports games?

I suddenly become the world's best referee, which always requires me to stand still and observe.

777. My kids asked why I'm always stretching before a game.

Because I need to prepare my 'dad muscles' for their biggest workout of the year.

778. Why do I always complain about my 'old sports injuries'?

Because without those old injuries, I'd have to admit that I'm just out of shape for no good reason.

779. My wife asked why I pretend to be a professional athlete.

Because I can't let go of the dream of being *that* dad at the game.

780. How do I feel after a family sports game?

Exhausted, sore, but secretly proud of winning.

781. My kids asked why I always say "back in my day..."

because it's totally believable that I was basically an elite athlete back in the day.

782. Why do I always talk about my 'glory days' in sports?

Because if I keep repeating it, maybe I'll start believing too.

783. My mate asked why I always call myself the "goal

master".

Because nothing says "goal master" like missing half the shots and then blaming it on 'the wind.

784. What's my excuse for not doing all the hard exercises?

I'll just cheer from the sidelines and claim I'm a 'motivational coach'.

785. My kids asked why I always say "I used to be in shape".

Because "used to" is a very flexible term when you're a dad.

786. Why do I make every family sports game feel like a championship match?

Because I believe in 'raising the stakes'—even if those stakes are just bragging rights until dinner.

787. My wife asked why I always insist on coaching.

Because every family needs a self-appointed expert who once played in high school and thinks they know everything about the game.

788. How do I feel when I lose a game?

Like I've let down my entire imaginary sports career.

789. My kids asked why I'm always trying to beat them at sports.

Because it's totally normal for a grown man to need validation from beating a couple of kids at tag.

790. What's my strategy for family sports games?

Make sure I win—then pretend it's all for fun.

791. My wife asked why I always say, "We'll get them next time".

because it sounds better than "Well, that went terribly wrong!"

792. How do I feel when I win at family sports?

Like I've just won the World Cup—except the trophy is a cookie.

793. My kids asked why I always say, "I'm just getting started".

Because I need them to know I still have a few 'tricks up my sleeve'—even if those tricks involve taking a break to catch my breath.

794. Why do I always act like a professional referee?

I like to think that if I ref well enough, someone will eventually hire me for a real gig. Until then, I'm just shouting at kids in the backyard.

795. My mate asked why I always say I'm the best player on the field.

It's funnier that way—especially when I trip over my own feet right after making that bold claim.

796. How do I make sports interesting for the kids?

By adding a 'twist'—like making every goal worth ten points if you do a silly dance afterward.

797. My kids asked why I always insist on playing.

I just love embarrassing myself in front of my entire family.

798. Why do I always talk about my 'unstoppable moves'?

Because if I don't hype myself up, who else is going to? —Certainly not the kids who've seen me miss a goal from two feet away.

799. My wife asked why I always make up random rules.

Because in my mind, I'm running an official league—The Dad Rules League—where random rules are the only rules that matter.

800. How do I feel after a losing a game against the kids?

Like a true underdog—except in this story, the underdog doesn't make an epic comeback, he just limps back to the couch.

Car Catastrophes

Ah, the open road—a place where Dads transform into navigational experts, mechanics, and occasionally, backseat referees. From the art of parallel parking (or not) to turning every road trip into a dramatic saga of snacks and wrong turns, cars are the ultimate stage for Dad hilarity.

This chapter celebrates the chaos of car rides, the triumph of finding a great parking spot, and the eternal Dad debate: "Do we really need to stop for directions?" Buckle up, because these jokes will have you laughing in the fast lane (or at least the slow lane, depending on traffic).

801. My kids asked why I always yell at the GPS.

I'm not yelling—I'm simply raising my voice to educate it on my superior sense of direction.

802. How do I know I'm a great driver?

Because even when I hit the curb, I do it with style—bonus points for making the whole family bounce!

803. My wife asked why I always insist on driving.

Because it's the only time I can pretend to be in control of something.

804. Why do I think I'm a parking expert?

Because I only need one try... if you don't count the other five 'adjustments' I make afterward.

805. My kids asked why I always say "We'll make it on time".

Because I need them to believe I have *some* idea where we're going.

806. How do I handle long road trips?

By convincing myself that "Are we there yet?" is actually a motivational chant—if you hear it enough times, it almost sounds like support.

807. My mate asked why I'm always the one to drive.

Because I love hearing everyone else's driving advice—makes me feel like I'm part of a driving academy.

808. What's my favourite part of a road trip?

Finding the perfect rest stop, even if it's just to stretch and pretend I'm not actually lost.

809. My kids asked why I always take the longest route.

I like to imagine we're in a travel documentary—taking in all the 'majestic' views of suburban streets and roundabouts.

810. How do I survive a long car ride with the kids?

It's a breeze—especially when they all need the bathroom... at completely different times.

811. My wife asked why I always try to navigate without directions.

Because nothing says 'Dad' like stubbornly refusing to ask for help.

812. Why do I always get nervous when I'm the passenger?

Because every time I'm the passenger, I suddenly become hyper-aware of how fragile life is—yet somehow, when I drive, we're immortal.

813. My kids asked why I always complain about "wasting time" at the gas station.

Because I need to make up for all the time I wasted taking to get here.

814. How do I make sure the kids don't argue in the car?

By playing their favourite songs on repeat—yes, even if it means listening to 'Baby Shark' so many times I start questioning my life choices.

815. My mate asked why I always turn off the radio when I'm lost.

Because nothing feels more like a Dad moment than silence while I figure out how to avoid looking like I don't know where I'm going.

816. What's my strategy for getting out of the driveway?

By convincing myself I can do it in one smooth motion—then making at least five adjustments to avoid taking out the recycling bins.

817. My wife asked why I always have a snack stash in the car.
I pack snacks for the kids but I end up eating most of them myself—call it dad tax!

818. How do I deal with traffic?
By loudly sighing and pretending I'm the only one suffering.

819. My kids asked why I always bring extra snacks on a trip.
Because someone's always going to drop their snack, spill their juice, or decide they suddenly hate raisins. Backup snacks save the day!

820. My kids asked why do I always go through drive-thru?
Because I like to pretend we're on a secret mission, and my orders are codewords—'Big Mac' is obviously classified information!

821. My wife asked why I always complain about parking.
Because no matter how great the spot is, someone's always too close, or too far.

822. How do I know I'm a dad driver?
When I see a space, and my first thought is, "I can fit in there... eventually".

823. My kids asked why I always talk to other drivers, even though they can't hear me.
Because I'm convinced I'm making the world a better place, one unheard piece of advice at a time.

824. Why do I love taking the car for a spin?

Because I like to imagine I'm in a car commercial—wind in my hair, music blasting, and a dramatic voice-over telling me I'm unstoppable.

825. How do I survive driving through bad weather?

By telling myself the car has magic powers—if I keep talking to it nicely, it'll keep all four wheels on the road.

826. My wife asked why I insist on using the air conditioner even when it's not hot.

Because without the AC, my dramatic sighs would fog up the windows.

827. Why do I refuse to stop for directions?

Because as a Dad, I'm *always* 10 minutes away from knowing exactly where I'm going.

828. My kids asked why I refuse to use GPS.

Because I think I'm still living in a world where 'just follow the signs' works.

829. How do I feel when I finally find a parking spot?

Like I've won the lottery and immediately start celebrating.

830. My wife asked why I always take forever to park.

Because I'm trying to park perfectly straight... in a world full of crookedly parked cars—call me a rebel!

831. Why do I always ask my wife if I can make a U-turn?

Because no major life decision—like changing direction—should be made without consulting the real boss of the car.

832. My kids asked why I can't just let them drive.

Unless you can magically grow a foot taller in the next five minutes to reach the pedals, I'm afraid the answer is no.

833. How do I deal with the car stereo system?

By pretending I know how to work the Bluetooth, even though I'm still struggling with the AUX cable.

834. My wife asked why I always have random stuff in the car.

Because I believe the car gets lonely, and all those random things are its little friends to keep it company.

835. Why do I always insist on driving with the windows down?

Because I'm secretly training everyone for an upcoming wind endurance competition—whoever can handle the breeze without complaints wins.

836. How do I make the kids appreciate a car ride?

By pretending we're on a grand adventure—'Next stop, the magical land of... Grandma's house!' It adds a little drama to the trip.

837. My mate asked why I always take the long route.

Because sometimes getting lost is more fun than the actual destination.

838. Why do I refuse to take the highway?

Because I like spending quality time with my family—in traffic, surrounded by every red light in town

839. My kids asked why I never trust the the radio.

Because last time I trusted it, I ended up with an hour of static and a talk show about cat grooming tips.

840. How do I feel after a long road trip?
Like I've just conquered the world.

841. My wife asked why I always make her navigate.
Because I'm trying to keep the drive interesting—what's a car ride without some quality 'are you sure that's the right turn?' banter.

842. Why do I always pretend to know a shortcut?
Because if I say it with enough confidence, maybe it'll actually be one.

843. How do I deal with backseat drivers?
By pretending they're not giving me directions, just 'helpful suggestions'.

844. My mate asked why I insist on taking my car everywhere.
Because I've convinced myself that I'm a better driver than I actually am.

845. Why do I get so proud when I find parking quickly?
Because it feels like winning a race I didn't know I was in.

846. My kids asked why I always tell them to "sit still" in the car.
Because a moving target is just too much to deal with while trying to navigate.

847. What's my strategy for a smooth car ride?

Drive like I'm in a movie, just hoping there's no plot twist... like traffic.

848. My wife asked why I always take the longest route home.

Because in my mind, every detour is an adventure.

849. Why do I act like a car expert?

Because sometimes, I can convince myself I know what I'm talking about—until something actually breaks.

850. How do I feel after a successful parking job?

Like I've just completed a high-stakes mission and totally nailed it.

Well done, you've made it halfway through the *Car Catastrophes* chapter! By now, you're probably thinking: *"I can totally handle this!"* after all those driving victories, parking successes, and snack-packed road trips. But let's be real, there's more to come. From yelling at the GPS to playing backseat referee during every family trip, you've already lived through the chaos of navigating the open road—just remember, this is the fun half! Whether it's still figuring out how to parallel park without causing a scene, or trying to stay calm while the kids argue about which song to play for the 100th time, buckle up: the second half of this journey promises even more unexpected detours, parking lot triumphs, and a whole lot of dad-powered driving! Let's hit the road again, and hope we don't take another wrong turn.

851. My wife asked why I always get so stressed when parking.

Because every time I'm about to park, I hear the theme song from *Mission Impossible* in my head.

852. How do I prepare for a road trip?

By making sure the car is stocked with snacks, drinks, and *at least* three backup plans for when we inevitably get lost.

853. My kids asked why I always take the longest route home.

Because I believe in the scenic route... even if it's just the freeway with more exits.

854. Why do I think I'm great at navigating?

Because I've mastered the art of pretending I know exactly where I'm going—until I don't.

855. My wife asked why I'm always so confident in my driving.

Because nothing says "I've got this" like pretending I can read a map while driving.

856. How do I make every car ride feel like an adventure?

By loudly declaring, "We're lost, but I know exactly where we are!" even when I don't.

857. My kids asked why I always have snacks in the car.

Because a snack-filled car is a happy car—especially when we're stuck in traffic.

858. Why do I insist on driving everywhere?

Because if I'm not behind the wheel, I can't pretend I know where we're going.

859. My mate asked why I keep a random assortment of tools in the car.

Because you never know when you'll need to perform 'Dad-level' car repairs, even if it's just to fix a loose cup holder.

860. How do I stay calm in traffic?

By pretending my horn is just a friendly "hello" to the person in front of me. Very loud, very friendly.

861. My wife asked why I refuse to stop for directions.

Because asking for directions is a dad's way of admitting defeat, and that's just not happening.

862. Why do I always get so defensive when someone else drives?

Because I'm convinced I'm the only one who knows how to navigate a roundabout properly.

863. My kids asked why I make a big deal about finding parking.

Because when you find a good spot, it feels like you've won the lottery. And who's not going to celebrate that?

864. How do I deal with backseat complainers?

By dramatically turning up the radio until I can't hear anything but the sweet sound of my own terrible singing.

865. My wife asked why I always use my 'dad voice' to give directions.

Because if I don't sound authoritative, how will anyone believe I'm in control?

866. Why do I always claim I can park a car in any spot?

Because it's a matter of pride—whether it takes one smooth move or a million small corrections, I'll get it done!

867. How do I handle wrong turns?

By declaring, "It's just a shortcut!", even if I'm 20 miles off course.

868. My kids asked why I always say "This is my last trip for the day".

I believe if I say it with enough conviction, the universe might actually listen.

869. Why do I pretend to know the best parking spots?

Because if you act confident enough, people start believing you.

870. My wife asked why I can't just 'relax' when I drive.

Because 'relaxing' behind the wheel is a myth only found in movies.

871. How do I survive road trips with the kids?

By being the snack distributor and pretending that the back-seat isn't in chaos.

872. My kids asked why I always take the longest route to avoid traffic.

I don't sitting bumper-to-bumper while someone in the next car picks their nose.

873. How do I know I'm an expert driver?

Because even though I sometimes miss an exit, I do it with such flair that it looks intentional.

874. My kids asked why I always check the oil, even though the car is brand new.

I like to pretend I'm a pit crew chief, making sure everything's perfect before our grand grocery store journey."

875. How do I prepare for a family trip?

By packing snacks, a first-aid kit, and a healthy dose of "we might get lost, but that's fine" optimism.

876. My wife asked why I'm always the one to get out of the car during a traffic jam.

Because I'm convinced my 'Dad powers' can somehow fix whatever's causing the jam. Spoiler alert: they can't

877. Why do I always pretend to be calm while driving?

Because I need to maintain my 'dad's in control' image—even if I'm silently panicking.

878. My kids asked why I always use the GPS, even when I know the way.

Because sometimes the GPS knows where the traffic is—and I'd rather avoid spending extra time bonding in the car with all of you!

879. How do I make sure the kids enjoy a long car ride?

By telling them there will be 'fun' stops along the way, even if the fun is just getting out to stretch.

880. My wife asked why I always say "I got this" when driving somewhere new.

Because I think the car runs better on pure overconfidence—keeps the engine and my ego running smoothly.

881. Why do I insist on driving everywhere?

Because it's the only time I feel like I'm truly in charge of my destiny. And also because I've mastered the art of 'car karaoke'.

882. My wife asked why I'm so obsessed with getting the car in just the right parking spot.

Because that perfect spot is a victory I can brag about for days.

883. How do I handle kids arguing in the backseat?

By offering to settle the debate like any rational adult: with a coin toss.

884. My kids asked why I insist on always 'testing the brakes'.

Because it's my way of making sure everyone is still awake—nothing like a little jolt to bring the car to life!

885. Why do I think I'm the only one who can read the road signs properly?

Because road signs were clearly designed with only my superior sense of direction in mind—everyone else is just guessing.

886. How do I know when we're lost?

When everyone in the car suddenly becomes a navigation expert... and none of it makes sense.

887. My wife asked why I insist on 'checking the tyre pres-

sure'.

Because nothing beats the thrill of squatting down, staring at the tire, and pretending I know what I'm doing.

888. Why do I always take the long scenic route on purpose?

I'm starring in my own nature documentary—*"And here we see a dad taking his family on a journey they definitely didn't ask for"*.

889. My kids asked why I can't drive without singing.

I've been told my driving is so good, it needs its own soundtrack—I'm just giving it the musical attention it deserves.

890. How do I feel after a successful road trip?

Like I deserve a trophy for managing to keep everyone alive, fed, and only slightly annoyed with each other.

891. My wife asked why I always 'rearrange' the car's interior for every trip.

Because I refuse to be caught unprepared for a sudden need to access a water bottle, map, or the emergency gummy bears.

892. Why do I always act like I'm in a car commercial?

Because in a car commercial, no one's asking, "Are we there yet?".

893. My kids asked why I insist on 'making a game' out of every traffic light.

Because turning the mundane into a competition is what dads do best.

894. Why do I always pack the car like it's the last trip I'll ever make?

Because if I'm going on a trip, I'm going *prepared*—snacks, blankets, and all.

895. How do I survive a road trip with a full car?

By pretending I'm driving a luxury bus with a very specific set of snack options.

896. My wife asked why I always insist on being the driver.

"Because I like to *steer* the situation"—here all week.

897. Why do I always get so defensive when someone suggests I take a shortcut?

Because there's nothing like a nice detour that adds 20 extra minutes to our trip..

898. How do I handle a flat tyre?

By trying to act like I totally know what I'm doing while secretly hoping someone else will pull over and offer to help.

899. My kids asked why I always get so obsessed with car maintenance.

Because I want to make sure nothing 'brakes' down unexpectedly—keeping everything in 'gear' is important.

900. How do I feel after the school run?

I feel great—there's nothing like starting the day with the chaos of missing shoes, last-minute lunches, and 15 different instructions on how to drive.

Shopping Struggles

Shopping—it's more than just a chore; it's a battlefield where Dads fight to save money, avoid impulse buys, and survive the checkout line with dignity intact. From debating the merits of generic vs. name-brand to attempting to 'carry it all in one' trip, shopping is where we truly shine (or fail spectacularly).

This chapter celebrates the quirks of shopping with Dad: the cart-pushing debates, the endless search for the best deals, and the occasional moment of triumph when we find something on sale *and* useful. Grab your reusable bags—it's time to laugh your way through the aisles!

901. My wife asked why I always end up with extra stuff at the checkout.

Because I'm just *that* good at finding 'must-have' items, even if they're not on the list.

902. How do I feel when I find something on sale?

Like I've just discovered treasure... even if it's a 50% off kitchen gadget I'll never use.

903. My kids asked why I always take forever to pick the right cereal.

Because picking cereal is an art form, and I'm trying to make the right choice for the family's breakfast legacy.

904. Why do I always end up buying more than I need at the store?

Because I'm convinced that if I don't buy it now, it will disappear forever, never to be seen again.

905. My wife asked why I always act like I'm getting a deal.

Because I'm *sure* that buying five bags of chips is a better idea than just one.

906. How do I survive shopping with kids?

By telling them that every item in the cart is "just for fun" until I'm at the checkout.

907. My wife asked why I always insist on paying with exact change.

I just love holding up the line while I count out pennies.

908. Why do I insist on carrying everything in one trip?

Because if I drop it, at least I can pretend I was *really* determined to get it all inside.

909. My kids asked why I always complain about the prices.

Because I'm a dad, and it's kind of my job to complain about how everything is overpriced.

910. What's my strategy when I'm stuck in a long line at

checkout?

I start judging the person in front of me who *clearly* doesn't know how to pack their items efficiently.

911. My wife asked why I always insist on going to the store during peak hours.

Because I'm trying to get the full 'shopping experience', including the thrill of squeezing through crowded aisles.

912. How do I feel when I miraculously manage to stick to the shopping list?

Like a hero in a world full of distractions and impulse buys.

913. My kids asked why I always try to squeeze the cart down the narrowest aisles.

Because if it fits, I'm convinced it'll help me get out faster, even if it's a tight squeeze.

914. Why do I always debate the difference between generic and name-brand?

Because I can't help but feel like a budget-conscious expert when I pick the store-brand pasta.

915. My wife asked why I get so invested in finding the best deals.

Because *finding a deal* is the ultimate victory in a dad's shopping game.

916. How do I deal with shopping carts that never cooperate?

By pretending that the one with the squeaky wheel has more character than the others.

917. My kids asked why I always look at the price tag so carefully.

Because I'm doing the maths in my head to figure out if I'm actually saving money or just spending more on snacks.

918. What's my strategy for avoiding impulse buys?

I pretend to put everything back on the shelf, but secretly buy it anyway when no one's looking.

919. My mate asked why I always seem to buy the weirdest things at the store.

Because when I see a good deal, my inner hoarder takes over.

920. How do I survive a trip to the grocery store?

By pretending I know where everything is, even though I'm always lost in the aisles.

921. My wife asked why I take forever to pick out vegetables.

Because I'm just trying to make sure I 'carrot' about quality—no one likes a bad apple.

922. Why do I act like I'm in the middle of a major decision when picking toilet paper?

Because I don't want to make a 'rough' choice and regret it later.

923. My kids asked why I always grab the cart with the broken wheel.

Because I like to live on the edge and test my shopping skills.

924. What's my shopping strategy when I'm really trying to

save money?

I only get what's on sale... even though I know I'll end up buying something I don't need.

925. My wife asked why I always insist on carrying all the heavy stuff.

Because if I can't handle the weight of my shopping choices, what kind of dad am I?

926. How do I know I'm not the *only* one shopping in the store?

Because I can hear other people also groaning about the prices—misery loves company.

927. My kids asked why I never let them buy sweets.

Because I like your teeth just the way they are—and so does the dentist.

928. Why do I act like I'm *really* good at couponing?

Because I like to pretend that clipping coupons makes me a shopping expert, even though I still forget to use them.

929. My mate asked why I always look at the 'clearance' section.

Because it's the treasure hunt part of shopping, and I'm always hoping for a steal.

930. How do I feel when I find a great deal on a random item?

Like I've just won the jackpot... even though I have no idea what Ive bought.

931. My wife asked why I never check the expiration date.

I love the thrill of wondering whether I've bought fresh milk or surprise yogurt.

932. How do I make sure the kids don't grab everything off the shelves?

I use the classic dad trick: "If you can carry it, you can have it". (Spoiler: They never carry it.)

933. Why do I always look for discounts even on non-essential items?

Because deep down, I think I'm saving money for the future... even though I never use any of it.

934. My wife asked why I always get so distracted by 'as seen on TV' products.

Because in my head, I'm already imagining how much better life will be with a pizza cutter that also peels potatoes.

935. How do I feel when I find a perfect deal?

Like I've just won a championship—only my prize is a box of discount cereal.

936. My kids asked why I always insist on buying 'one more thing'.

Because every dad knows that 'one more thing' is a *necessity*.

937. How do I survive the endless aisles?

By treating it like an endurance sport, where the prize at the end is a discounted pack of socks.

938. My wife asked why I always seem to forget the most important item on the list.

Because, in my defence, I was distracted by the 2-for-1 deal on something I'll never use.

939. How do I handle a crowded store?

By acting like I'm an expert in navigating tight spaces and pretending I'm not at my wit's end.

940. My kids asked why I always complain about prices when I know I'm still buying stuff.

Because a dad's gotta keep up the facade of 'being careful with money', even if I'm still buying extra snacks.

941. Why do I get so proud when I get the last item on a shelf?

Because when you're a dad, securing the last jar of pickles feels like a *major* accomplishment.

942. My mate asked why I always grab a basket instead of a cart.

Because I like the challenge of fitting *everything* into a basket, even though it never works.

943. How do I feel about impulse buys?

Like I'm *definitely* getting something useful... until I get home and realize it's just a cute pen holder.

944. My wife asked why I always check for coupons at checkout.

Because if I don't, I'll be haunted by the *one* missed opportunity to save a little.

945. Why do I always act like I'm a 'savvy shopper'?
Because I read one article on shopping hacks and now feel like a professional.

946. My kids asked why I always buy the same snacks.
Because I've found my favourites—and I'm not about to be swayed by trendy snack fads.

947. How do I deal with impulse buys?
By convincing myself that "It's on sale! I *have* to get it now!"

948. My wife asked why I always seem to get a little too excited about discounts.
Because finding a good deal makes me feel like I've just won a prize.

949. Why do I always get so attached to my shopping cart?
Because I've been pushing it around the store for so long, it feels like part of the family.

950. My kids asked why I always leave the store feeling 'accomplished'.
Because I'm convinced I've just secured the best deals of the day—even if they were for things I didn't need.

Congratulations, you've officially made it halfway through the Shopping Struggles chapter! By now, you've probably mastered the art of pretending that buying a random kitchen gadget on sale was a necessary purchase and that your extensive search for the best deal was a strategic move. But don't get too comfortable—there's still plenty of shopping chaos ahead! Whether you're racing to get in and out of the store in record time or convincing yourself that 10 bags of chips are absolutely essential, the second half of this chapter will have you laughing your way down the aisles (or trying to squeeze your cart into tight spaces). Keep your reusable bags handy because the shopping game is far from over—trust me, you're going to need them for all the impulse buys, hidden treasures, and 'emergency' items that await.

951. Why do I always make a list before I go shopping?

Because if I don't, I'll end up with three bottles of ketchup and no bread.

952. How do I avoid impulse buys at checkout?

By pretending the last-minute items are for 'emergency use'—which I never actually need.

953. My wife asked why I always take so long in the store.

Because I'm conducting thorough research on every product... even the ones I don't buy.

954. Why do I always check the unit price on everything?

Because I'm determined to figure out the *real* cost of that 5-pack of toilet paper.

955. How do I handle seeing something I *really* want at the store?

I remind myself that my credit card bill is already big enough to be a family heirloom.

956. My mate asked why I always grab the first item off the shelf.

Because I'm pretending I'm in a grocery store challenge and need to make quick decisions.

957. How do I justify buying something I don't need?

By convincing myself that it's 'on sale'—even if it's 50% off a product I'll never use.

958. Why do I always take the longest route through the store?

Because I'm convinced that if I walk every aisle, I'll find that 'perfect' deal.

959. My kids asked why I always pick the store-brand snacks.

Because I'm living on a budget, and my taste buds have learned to adjust.

960. How do I deal with buying more than I intended?

I tell myself, "It's a bulk purchase—it's basically saving money, right?"

961. Why do I check my shopping cart 10 times before checking out?

Because I'm making sure I haven't accidentally purchased something ridiculous—like 30 cans of beans.

962. My wife asked why I always ask for a gift receipt.

Because I'm secretly hoping to return half of it later.

963. How do I survive a trip to a store I don't like?

By treating it like an obstacle course, where the prize is a discount on toilet paper.

964. Why do I buy snacks I don't need?
Because my kids' cries of "Dad, can we get this?" make me feel like a hero—until we get home.

965. How do I manage my shopping cart during a sale?
By filling it to the brim, then convincing myself I'm saving *so much money* on stuff I don't even need.

966. Why do I insist on buying everything in bulk?
Because 'more is always better'—until I realize I've got enough pasta to last a lifetime.

967. My mate asked why I always get the self-checkout.
Because I like to pretend I'm saving time, even though I'm just scanning one item at a time.

968. How do I deal with the urge to buy something random?
I tell myself, "I'm just expanding my horizons".

969. Why do I always check the weekly flyers before going to the store?
Because I believe there's a hidden treasure in every deal... even if it's just 10% off cereal.

970. How do I survive shopping with a cart full of kids?
By pretending they're not touching everything and hoping the checkout line is quick.

971. My wife asked why I bought 10 bags of chips.

"They're on sale! and I'm convinced we'll need them for the apocalypse".

972. How do I stay calm at the store?

By reminding myself that the extra snacks are just 'strategic purchases'—for later.

973. Why do I always go to the store when I'm hungry?

Because I'm convinced that if I buy everything in sight, I'll feel less hungry.

974. How do I try to avoid spending too much at the store?

By convincing myself that I'll only buy essentials—and then leaving with a reusable bag full of 'non-essentials'.

975. My mate asked why I always get so excited when I see a sale.

Because in my mind, I'm a treasure hunter finding hidden gold.

976. How do I deal with a store's 'limited-time offer'?

By buying things I don't need because I'm convinced the deal will disappear in 5 minutes.

977. Why do I always shop at the same store?

Because I know the layout like the back of my hand... even though I still get lost every time.

978. My wife asked why I never use the shopping trolley.

Because I believe the real challenge is carrying everything in my hands.

979. How do I avoid regret after shopping?

By telling myself that "it's all part of the adventure"—even if it's just socks on sale.

980. Why do I insist on shopping at discount stores?

Because I believe that saving a few pounds is the real reward, even if I don't need half of what I buy.

981. My kids asked why I always look at the price per unit.

Because I'm a *master* at getting the best deal... even if it's on stuff we don't use.

982. How do I handle shopping during the holiday season?

By pretending it's an Olympic event and I'm the gold medallist of last-minute shopping.

983. Why do I always buy more food than I need?

You never know when the apocalypse 'might' happen, for which I'll need 5 years worth of peanut butter.

984. How do I feel after a successful shopping trip?

Like I've conquered the world—until I see the credit card bill.

985. My wife asked why I always end up buying items we don't need.

Because in my head, they're 'essentials' for life's survival.

986. Why do I always buy snacks before a road trip?

Because I'm convinced the journey isn't complete without a 10-pound bag of trail mix.

987. How do I shop for my kids?

By letting them pick what they want, then pretending it's a 'life lesson' on decision-making.

988. My mate asked why I always get a shopping cart even when I only have 5 items.

Because the cart is *my territory*, and I'm not afraid to claim it.

989. How do I make sure I'm not tempted by impulse buys?

By filling my cart with essentials... until I'm at the checkout and realize what I've done.

990. Why do I always feel the need to get everything 'on sale'?

Because the thrill of a deal is too strong to resist—even if I'm just getting 5 more boxes of cereal.

991. How do I handle finding an item I *really* want in the store?

I try to convince myself I *don't* need it, but my cart disagrees.

992. My wife asked why I buy so much frozen food.

Because I'm a gourmet chef who works in the fine art of reheating and defrosting.

993. How do I survive a store with way too many choices?

By reminding myself that every product claims to be 'the best'.

994. My wife asked why I never go to the store with a plan.

Because if I go with a plan, I have something to forget.

995. How do I handle going to a store I don't like?

I just keep my head down, avoid eye contact with the chaos, and hope I can find the checkout before my patience runs out.

996. My kids asked why I always get excited about sales.

Because in my head, I'm the hero who just saved the family a *fortune*.

997. How do I handle shopping during busy hours?

By pretending I'm in a race and speed-walking through the aisles.

998. My wife asked why I always pick up random things at the checkout.

Because in my mind, they're 'emergency items' I'll never use.

999. How do I avoid buyer's remorse?

By telling myself "I saved so much money!"

1000. Why do I always check the sale racks first?

Because if I find something cheap enough, I can justify everything else I buy.

The Grand Finale: The 1001st Dad Joke

Ladies and gentlemen, children and adults, family members who roll their eyes at every Dad joke... We've reached the peak. The 1001st joke. The joke to end all jokes. You've laughed, you've groaned, and you've probably whispered, 'Please, Dad, no more.' But here it is, the grand crescendo of this epic journey into Dad humour. Buckle up, because this one's going to hit harder than a wobbly shopping cart in the frozen food aisle!

This is the joke Dads will whisper with reverence, the one that will echo through generations. It's the culmination of spilled coffee, broken shelves, and road trip catastrophes. It's the joke that unites us all in the universal truth: Dads are the undisputed kings of comedy. Buckle up, folks—this one's going to hit harder than a wobbling shopping cart at full speed.

Picture this: the family gathered around the dinner table, forks poised in mid-air, eyes rolling so far back you'd think they were stuck. Somewhere, amidst the chorus of groans and muffled laughter, comes the inevitable cry of our time: *"Dad, Stop!"*

You see, Dad jokes are more than just punchlines—they're a test of endurance, a game of wit, and a declaration of unconditional love disguised as cringe-worthy comedy. Every "Dad, Stop" is a badge of honour, a reminder that no matter how bad the joke, it's been heard, felt, and begrudgingly appreciated.

So here we are at the grand finale. This isn't just another joke—it's the perfect encapsulation of the entire journey. It's the groan heard 'round the world, the line that will echo through generations, bringing laughter, a little eye-rolling, and maybe—just maybe—a moment of true Dad brilliance.

The 1001st Joke

1001. Why do my kids keep shouting "Dad, Stop"?
Because they secretly love every cringe-worthy second.

And there it is—the 1001st joke, the pièce de résistance of Dad humour. It perfectly encapsulates everything a dad joke stands for: the relentless pursuit of laughter, even when it's met with groans, eye-rolls, and possibly a dramatic exit from the room. But don't worry, dear reader, that groan isn't a complaint—it's a compliment! After all, if your joke doesn't make people roll their eyes, did you even *really* tell a Dad joke? Every "Dad, Stop!" is just a cleverly disguised cheer for your commitment to the craft.

So, what's next? Go forth, armed with your new Dad joke arsenal, and proudly tell your jokes, no matter the audience. Wear your "Dad, Stop" like a medal of honour, because that's exactly what it is—a badge that shows you're not just a dad, you're a warrior in the battle for laughter. And if no one laughs at your joke, well, don't sweat it—just take a bow, because somewhere, someone is secretly smiling (probably in the next room, pretending not to hear). Keep telling those jokes, and remember, Dad humour is the gift that keeps on giving—whether they like it or not!

Thank you for joining this journey. Now, close the book, tell the joke, and watch the magic happen.

About the Author

Paul Murphy is a devoted connoisseur of Dad jokes, a champion of clever wordplay, and a self-proclaimed 'Master of Unsolicited Dad Humour'. When he's not delighting (or terrifying) his family with his latest one-liner, you'll find him plotting his next joke-filled escapade. His mission in life? To deliver the perfect punchline at the most unexpected—and often most inconvenient—moments.

Living with his ever-tolerant family, Paul holds the honorary title of 'Sultan of Silly Punchlines'. His family has learned to brace themselves when he enters the room, knowing full well that a dad joke is probably coming their way. But hey, if you can't laugh at a bad pun, what's the point of being a dad?

When he's not busy perfecting his comedic timing, Paul enjoys pretending he's a stand-up comedian in the living room, cracking himself up even if the audience (his family) is, let's say, a bit less enthusiastic. He believes that the best laughs come from the most groan-worthy moments, and if you're not rolling your eyes at least once a day, you're not doing it right.

Call to Action – Share the Laughs!

Congratulations, Groaner Extraordinaire!

You've made it to the end of *1001 Dad Jokes: Making "Dad, Stop" the Official Family Motto*. Whether you laughed out loud, cringed uncontrollably, or rolled your eyes so hard they got stuck (sorry about that), we hope this book brought a little extra humour to your day.

Here's how you can be a legend:

Leave a Review:

- Did one of the jokes make your kids groan louder than ever? Did you accidentally snort coffee while reading? Tell the world! A quick review helps other joke-lovers find this book and ensures that Dad humour remains alive and well.

Share Your Favourite Joke:

- Found a joke in here that's just too good to keep to yourself? Post it on social media, text it to a friend, or share it at the next family dinner. (We can't guarantee everyone will laugh, but that's the beauty of Dad jokes.)

Warning: This Series Is Highly Addictive!

If you enjoyed this book, the rest of the **1001 Series** is waiting for you, packed with more puns, quips, and dad moments that'll have you laughing (and maybe groaning) even more. Each book in the series is filled with jokes designed to brighten your day and provide the perfect excuse to roll your eyes in the most loving way possible.

Find the rest of the **1001 Series** here:

- **Amazon UK**: amazon.co.uk/dp/B0DNR8WRM3
- **Amazon US**: amazon.com/dp/B0DNR8WRM3
- **Amazon Canada**: amazon.ca/dp/B0DNR8WRM3
- **Amazon Australia**: amazon.com.au/dp/B0DNR8WRM3

Remember, it's a zero after the B—just like the number of times you'll stop telling dad jokes.

Until next time, keep spreading the laughs, passing on the puns, and making the world a little lighter, one Dad joke at a time.

Your Continued Mission (If You Choose to Accept It):

Carry on the Dad joke legacy. Whether you're a Dad, know a Dad, or just appreciate the art of terrible humour, you're now an honorary member of the "Dad Joke Hall of Fame".

Remember: Every groan is just laughter in disguise. Keep joking, keep laughing, and most importantly—keep spreading the "Dad, Stop" motto!

A Huge Thank You

From the bottom of our pun-loving hearts, thank you for joining us on this journey through *1001 Dad Jokes*. Whether you're a seasoned Dad joke veteran, an aspiring pun master, or just someone who appreciates the art of a good groan, this book wouldn't have come alive without you.

Your laughs (and eye rolls) are the reason this collection exists. Sharing these jokes with your family, friends, and anyone who will listen keeps the spirit of Dad humour thriving. Every chuckle, groan, and whispered *"Dad, Stop"* is a victory for comedy everywhere.

This is just the beginning. Keep your eyes peeled for more books in the *1001* series. There are plenty more laughs, groans, and unexpected punchlines coming your way. Whether it's more puns, more fun, or even jokes that *Mom would approve of* — there's always another chapter of humour waiting to be written.

Thank you for being part of the *1001 Dad Jokes* family. See you in the next book!

Dedication to Dads Everywhere

This one's for the Dads.

For the Dads who can't resist a pun, even when the entire room groans in unison. For the Dads who bravely face eye rolls, smirks, and the dreaded *"Dad, Stop"* with unwavering pride. For the Dads who turn every awkward silence into an opportunity to deliver the ultimate punchline.

This is for the Dads who make grocery store trips a comedy show, who can't resist turning everyday objects into props for their latest bit, and who believe every family dinner needs at least one good groan-worthy laugh.

To the Dads who know that humour isn't about getting the biggest laugh—it's about connecting. It's about creating memories, sparking joy, and showing love in the quirkiest, most unexpected ways.

This book is dedicated to you—the kings of cringe, the sultans of silly, and the heroes of humour. Thank you for reminding us that the best jokes aren't about perfection—they're about making the people you love smile, even if they're trying not to.

Keep groaning, keep laughing, and most importantly, keep

being you.

Printed in Great Britain
by Amazon

53019289R00090